METRO BOOKS
New York

An Imprint of Sterling Publishing Co., Inc.
1166 Avenue of the Americas
New York, NY 10036

ISBN 978-1-4351-6661-5

For information about custom editions, special sales, and premium and
corporate purchases, please contact Sterling Special Sales at 800-805-5489
or specialsales@sterlingpublishing.com.

Manufactured in Singapore

6 8 10 9 7 5

sterlingpublishing.com

Credits: Design and illustration by Mike Lebihan

UNSOLVED CRIMES

INFAMOUS CASES THAT HAVE
PUZZLED THE GREATEST MINDS

SARAH HERMAN

METRO BOOKS
New York

CONTENTS

INTRODUCTION   6

MURDER   9

Did Napoleon Bonaparte die from arsenic poisoning?   10

Was Edgar Allan Poe murdered?   16

Did Lizzie Borden murder her father and stepmother
with an axe?   22

Who assassinated Michael Collins?   28

Was Al Capone behind the St. Valentine's Day massacre?   34

Who killed Sir Harry Oakes?   40

Who was responsible for the Black Dahlia murder?   44

Who was behind the assassination of Archbishop
Oscar Romero?   50

Who murdered the Italian banker Roberto Calvi?   54

Who killed Swedish Prime Minister Olof Palme?   60

Who killed hundreds of women in the Mexican city of
Ciudad Juárez?   66

Who killed JonBenét Ramsey?   70

Were the murders of Tupac Shakur and Biggie
Smalls connected?   76

Who ordered the murder of Anna Politkovskaya?   82

What is the explanation for the Salish Sea feet mystery?   88

TERRORISM   93

Who was responsible for the Wall Street bombing?   94

Who were the real Birmingham pub bombers?   100

Who was responsible for the East African
U.S. embassy bombings?   104

Who shot down Malaysia Airlines Flight 17 over Ukraine?   110

SERIAL KILLING   115

What was Jack the Ripper's real identity?   116

Who was the Axeman of New Orleans?   122

Who committed the Cleveland torso murders?   128

Who was the Zodiac Killer?   134

What was the identity of the Original Night Stalker?   140

Who was responsible for the Chicago Tylenol murders?   144

Why haven't police caught the Long Island serial killer?   148

ROBBERY AND FRAUD   153

Who stole the Irish Crown Jewels?   154

Who was the Mystery Man with 21 Faces?   160

Who robbed the Isabella Stewart Gardner Museum?   164

Who committed the Amsterdam diamond heist?   170

Who was behind the Banco Central robbery in Fortaleza, Brazil?   174

Who stole four masterpieces from a Zurich art museum?   180

Who committed the Carlton Hotel diamond heist?   184

UNEXPLAINED DISAPPEARANCES   191

What happened to Judge Crater?   192

What happened to the Alcatraz escapees?   198

Did Lord Lucan murder the family nanny and then
make his escape?   204

Why did Jimmy Hoffa disappear?   210

What happened to Madeleine McCann?   214

FURTHER READING   218
INDEX   220

INTRODUCTION

Thanks to today's modern technology and relentless investigators, cold cases don't necessarily stay cold forever. In these times of desktop detectives, where investigators the world over can access records, satellite imagery, and evidence online, there's more reason than not to believe an unsolved crime that's been dead in the water for some time might suddenly jolt back to life.

That said, many of the stories contained within these pages are famed and fretted over for the very fact they have never been settled. Some are the work of particularly cunning criminals, whose ability to cover their tracks has meant they've eluded even the most dedicated detectives. Some took place before advancements in fingerprinting and DNA evidence; they're crimes that, if they happened today, would be more easily solved (or not committed in the first place, for the sheer likelihood of getting caught). And then there are others that probably became unsolvable from the moment the police stepped on the scene.

Whether because of a police force's bad judgement or a criminal's ability to outwit the cops, the simple fact that those involved in these crimes are long dead and gone makes it harder to uncover new evidence and draw fresh conclusions. But from multimillion-dollar diamond heists and a serial killer in Victorian London, to the terrorist attack that wiped out Wall Street, we cannot help but be intrigued and wonder how the assailants did it—the ones who got away.

As any private detective will know, answering one question only leads to another. And this book asks a fair few questions. Whether it's the man and his wife found butchered by an axe-wielding murderer (surely it couldn't have been his loving daughter who dealt the fatal blows?) or a beautiful woman found cut in half in Hollywood and left by the side of the road (who had the surgical expertise to inflict her gruesome wounds?), the one thing all these cases have in common is

Right: The dirty work of death: police in Pittsburgh on the trail of the elusive "Butcher of Kingsbury Run."

the fact they're missing answers. Not to mention their notoriety. From the Chicago residents who started dropping dead after taking Tylenol, to the Cleveland-based killer who beheaded and dismembered his victims, there's not one story here that hasn't been told around the world, leaving millions wondering, who did that?

Public hearsay and media untruths imbued with the passion of the moment have led many of these cases astray; exaggeration and speculation doing little to help the police and everything to divert attention away from the real perpetrators. While an entire book would never be enough to fully analyze a single one of these cases, there are patterns that emerge by reading the facts of each case in turn: unsecured crime scenes, institutional conspiracy, not quite enough evidence to prosecute.

Soon enough, you find yourself playing detective, asking why that piece of evidence was disregarded, why that witness was never interviewed, and why that official was believed at their word. Before long, you realize these cases aren't so cold after all. They're just waiting for the right person to come along and warm them up.

MURDER

As DNA evidence and fingerprint databases have played an increasingly pivotal role in police work, committing a murder without leaving a trace of yourself for investigators to find has become harder and harder. Many of the unsolved murders in this section took place prior to the first uses of DNA evidence in court (1986 in the UK and 1987 in the USA), and some before fingerprints were admissible evidence (1911 in the USA). So it's not hard to imagine why the unexplained death of Edgar Allan Poe, the murders of Lizzie Borden's parents, and the case of the Black Dahlia were never solved. It's likely that with the crime scene investigation techniques in use today, these stories would have been open-and-shut cases.

Even with advanced technology, though, detectives have been unable to solve the more recent murders of Archbishop Oscar Romero, who was gunned down from his pulpit in San Salvador in 1980, or the assassination of Swedish prime minister Olof Palme in 1986 on the streets of Stockholm. In high-profile cases like these, where evidence is rife but no suspects emerge, questions of police incompetence and government corruption usually take the place of any official arrests and convictions. In the case of the St. Valentine's Day massacre in 1920s Chicago, where mistrust of law enforcement was already high, the killers even dressed as police officers. Sometimes the murderers will go to great lengths to remain secret, usually taking the ghastly truth of what they did to their grave.

Left: Murdered by the mob—the victims of the St. Valentine's Day Massacre, which took place in 1920s Chicago.

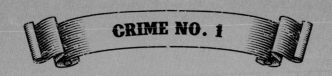
DID NAPOLEON BONAPARTE DIE FROM ARSENIC POISONING?

Date: May 5, 1821
Location: Saint Helena, South Atlantic

Napoleon may have commanded huge armies to unprecedented victories, but his military prowess couldn't protect him from an untimely death.

When he set foot on the shore of the isolated British island of Saint Helena on October 17, 1815, Napoleon Bonaparte was leaving behind the life of an emperor and stepping into his new role as a prisoner. After his disastrous defeat at the Battle of Waterloo, on June 18, 1815, Napoleon had abdicated the French throne and given himself up to the British. While he might have been hoping for exile in the United States, they decided the best place for him was this tiny island in the South Atlantic Ocean—the nearest land some 1,200 miles away.

Napoleon spent nearly six years living on Saint Helena, but after a period of illness, he died on May 5, 1821, at the age of fifty-two. The verdict from the autopsy carried out was that he had died from stomach cancer, like his father before him. A comprehensive study published in the journal *Nature Clinical Practice Gastroenterology and Hepatology* in 2007 confirmed that the reported evidence was consistent with a diagnosis of gastric cancer.

Most medical researchers are in agreement about the nature of Napoleon's demise, but there was something unusual about his corpse that points to a more sinister end. Was this cancerous death verdict covering up a plot to assassinate the Little Corporal?

ARSENIC IN HIS HAIR

In Napoleon's last will and testament, recorded just three weeks before his demise, he wrote: "I die before my time, murdered by the English oligarchy and its hired assassin." This foretelling has formed the basis for the belief that cancer was not what finished Napoleon off, but that one or more

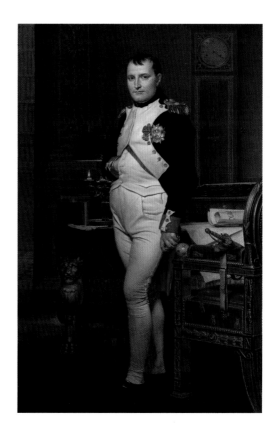

Above: Emperor Napoleon as painted by Jacques-Louis David in 1812, nine years before his death.

of his island companions plotted to assassinate him. There were many who wanted Napoleon dead: his French rivals, who feared he would return, yet again, to take the throne (Napoleon had previously escaped from the Mediterranean island of Elba, where he had been exiled after his forced abdication); and his enemies, the allied nations of Great Britain, Austria, Prussia, and Russia.

After the French King Charles X was overthrown by the people in 1830, the reign of Louis Philippe I began. The new monarch had had no quarrel with Napoleon, and so he started negotiations with the British to have Napoleon's body returned to France. In 1840 his body was exhumed from its resting place on Saint Helena and transported to Paris. When the soldiers sent to retrieve him opened the casket, they were shocked to discover a corpse that was almost

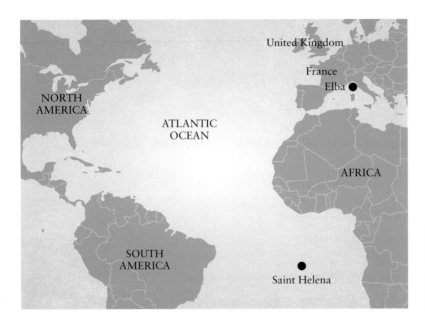

Left: Saint Helena sits 1,200 miles from the nearest mainland. Napoleon had previously been exiled to Elba, much closer to home.

perfectly preserved, despite the fact it hadn't been embalmed—a sign of severe alcohol, antimony, or arsenic poisoning. Because arsenic is toxic to microorganisms that would ordinarily break down human tissue, if there are large amounts of arsenic present, decomposition is significantly slowed—a phenomenon known as "arsenic mummification."

Over the years a number of experiments have been conducted on samples of Napoleon's hair to test for the presence of arsenic. During his lifetime he gave locks of hair as souvenirs to admirers and, when he died, in accordance with his wishes, his hair was cut off and distributed to various members of his establishment as keepsakes, providing further evidence for testing. The level of arsenic found in the samples, which are dated between 1805 and 1821, varies from 15 parts per million (ppm) to 100 ppm. A more normal level is 1 ppm, and 3 ppm is considered the maximum safe limit. These findings support the theory that throughout the last months of his life, Napoleon was exposed to high levels of arsenic.

FATAL FURNISHINGS

How did he come to have so much arsenic in his body? In the nineteenth century arsenic was actually a very common ingredient in medical remedies, fabrics, artificial plants, soaps, and paper products. Wallpaper and wallpaper paste contained arsenic as a deterrent for rats—a common problem, particularly at Longwood House where Napoleon resided on Saint Helena. A piece of green wallpaper from Napoleon's quarters was tested in the 1990s. (It had been torn from the walls not long after Napoleon's death by a visitor to the site in 1823 and kept in a scrapbook.) The sample was found to contain high levels of arsenic. It's possible that the island's typically wet and damp weather created the right conditions for mold to grow and release high levels of an arsenic-based gas called trimethylarsine into the atmosphere. This deadly decorative feature was a common sight throughout the 1800s—in the UK alone, one million rolls of wallpaper were sold each year by 1830. When tests were carried out toward the end of the century, four out of five wallpapers were found to contain arsenic.

Below: Longwood House on Saint Helena, where Napoleon spent almost all of his six-year exile.

While it's possible the high levels of arsenic found in Napoleon's hair samples contributed to his death, studies of other samples from his earlier life by physicists at the University of Milano-Bicocca and the University of Pavia, Italy, point to the fact that Napoleon had lived with these relatively high levels of arsenic since boyhood.

DO NO HARM

There's no denying Napoleon was sick before he died. The autopsy carried out after his death by his physician, Dr. François Carlo Antommarchi, and corroborated by five other doctors, named stomach cancer as the cause. However, research in recent years by a team at the San Francisco Medical Examiner's Department has shone a spotlight on the treatments he received. Their theory suggests the medicine that sought to make him better may actually have killed him off.

To alleviate the intermittent nausea Napoleon suffered from in the last eight months of his life, he was prescribed regular doses of antimony potassium tartrate, a poisonous colorless salt that induces vomiting. This would have caused a serious potassium deficiency, which could have led to a potentially fatal heart condition. This, coupled with the 600 mg—five times the normal dose—of mercuric chloride, or calomel as it is otherwise known, administered to him two days before he died to help clear his intestines, would have further reduced his body's potassium levels. However, calomel would also have masked the symptoms of arsenic poisoning if given to a victim shortly before their death. Perhaps this unusually large dose was a way to disguise the poisoner's actions?

Most doctors today agree that medical intervention may have hindered rather than helped Napoleon's condition, and that even if arsenic had been administered as a poison, he would have succumbed to his stomach cancer either way. He was a powerful man with many enemies, and no matter how he died, his death would have fueled conspiracy theories for centuries to come.

— STRANGE —
SUSPICION

While the autopsy result removed the need for any official murder investigation, historians have pointed the finger at a number of Saint Helena's residents. These include Dr. Antommarchi, who theorists believe was bribed by the French government to kill Napoleon. Also accused is Napoleon's jailer, Sir Hudson Lowe, who was worried his prisoner might try to escape.

A more convincing culprit is Comte Charles-Tristan de Montholon. The general was head of Napoleon's household, with access to his food and wine. It's thought that Montholon was blackmailed into administering regular doses of arsenic by the Comte d'Artois (who later became Charles X), a political rival of Napoleon's who wanted to ensure he'd never return to France. On top of this, Montholon's wife had had an affair with the emperor and he stood to gain from Napoleon's will. More pointedly, a book about the true story of Madame de Brinvilliers, a seventeenth-century French aristocrat who was

Above: Charles-Tristan de Montholon, war hero and Napoleon's trusted adviser, could have been the one to poison him.

convicted of poisoning three people, was found in the general's quarters.

But according to some, Montholon may not have been trying to poison his master at all—some think he was trying to make his patron sick enough to convince the British to let him leave the island.

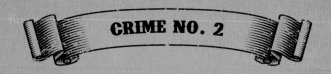

WAS EDGAR ALLAN POE MURDERED?

Date: October 7, 1849
Location: Baltimore, Maryland, USA

The story of Edgar Allan Poe's unsavory and inconclusive end includes gang beatings and rabies, but the true cause remains as mysterious and macabre as the stories he wrote.

On September 27, 1849, famed author Edgar Allan Poe left his fiancé, Elmira Shelton, in Richmond, Virginia, and headed north to New York, where he planned to meet his aunt and accompany her back to Richmond for his impending wedding. He'd arranged a pit stop in Philadelphia, where he had business editing a collection of poetry by a Mrs. St. Leon Loud. Unfortunately, Poe never made it that far. He broke his journey in Baltimore, and ten days later he was dead.

Poe reportedly met with friends on September 28 for drinks, but what happened in the days that followed is the stuff of mystery. On October 3, election day in the city, Joseph W. Walker, a local compositor for the *Baltimore Sun*, found him outside Gunner's Hall, an Irish pub being used as a ballot station. Poe was incoherent, shabbily dressed, and behaving like a drunk, but Walker recognized him and asked if he had any friends in the area.

Poe managed to offer up the name of a magazine editor he knew who lived nearby, named Joseph Snodgrass. Walker immediately penned him a note:

Dear Sir,
There is a gentleman, rather the worse for wear, at Ryan's 4th ward polls, who goes under the cognomen of Edgar A. Poe, and who appears in great distress, & he says he is acquainted with you, he is in need of immediate assistance.
Yours, in haste,
JOS. W. WALKER

Snodgrass would later recall the state he found his friend in, remarking on the man's attire, which Poe was usually so particular about: "His hat—or rather the hat of somebody else, for he had evidently been robbed of his clothing, or cheated in an exchange—was a cheap palm-leaf one … his coat … evidently 'second-hand'; his pants … dingy and badly fitting … while his shirt was sadly crumpled and soiled."

Above: Celebrated author Edgar Allan Poe in his usual formal attire, quite different from the clothes he was found wearing that night in 1849.

Poe was moved to Washington Medical College Hospital, where he arrived in a stupor. And by the early hours of October 4, he had grown more delirious. After three days passing in and out of consciousness, he died at 3 a.m. on October 7. His cause of death was reported in the *Baltimore Clipper* as "congestion of the brain," and no autopsy was performed. A rushed burial followed on October 8, organized by Poe's cousins and attended by only a few.

DRUNKEN DISASTER

Poe's behavior caused many to believe that he was drunk and that this, combined with his existing health problems, had

Above: The Edgar Allan Poe memorial at Westminster Hall, Baltimore, where the famous writer is buried with his wife and mother-in-law. Poe's funeral was attended by just a few people.

brought about his death. This theory was supported by his close friend J. P. Kennedy, who speculated three days later: "He fell in with some companion here who seduced him to the bottle … The consequence was fever, delirium, and madness." A few months prior to his death Poe had become a member of the temperance movement, abstaining from alcohol. He'd struggled with drinking in the past, particularly during the long illness of his first wife, and was known to have a strong reaction to even a small amount of alcohol. Snodgrass was also a member of the movement, and later used Poe's death to preach about the dangers of binge drinking.

There is debate, however, over whether Poe was drunk at all. Forty years later, Dr. John Moran, who treated him on October 6 and 7, published a biographical memoir stating that: "Edgar Allan Poe did not die under the effect of any intoxicant, nor was the smell of liquor upon his breath or person." He blamed the rumors of Poe's drunkenness on Rufus Griswold, a biographer and rival of Poe's. Poe's cousin, Rev. W. T. D. Clemm, who presided over his funeral, was confused and surprised by the physician's change of heart. In 1889 he wrote, "it positively contradicts the statement made to me personally by the Doctor."

POLITICAL COOP

Either way, drunkenness alone could not account for the shabby clothes he was found in. Maybe there was some foul play involved? The fact that Poe was found at a polling station for a municipal election feeds into one of the prevailing theories about his fate. At that time, elections were corrupt and violent. In a practice known as "cooping," would-be voters were kidnapped by gang members, beaten, force-fed alcohol, dressed in disguises, and made to vote for a specific candidate multiple times. In a 1930 book co-authored by sisters Elizabeth Ellicott Poe and Vylla Poe Wilson, Poe's first cousins once removed, the theory that he had been a victim of cooping prevailed: "The conclusion to be drawn ... is that he [Poe] was shanghaied shortly after his arrival in Baltimore, given liquor and opium ... and while in the irresponsible condition held until election day."

Below: Poe spent three days at Washington Medical College Hospital (now part of Georgetown University) drifting in and out of consciousness before he died.

Some have taken this theory further, arguing that Poe was the victim of a violent brawl or murder. In his 1998 book, *Midnight Dreary: The Mysterious Death of Edgar Allan Poe*, John Evangelist Walsh accuses Elmira Shelton's three brothers of ambushing Poe in

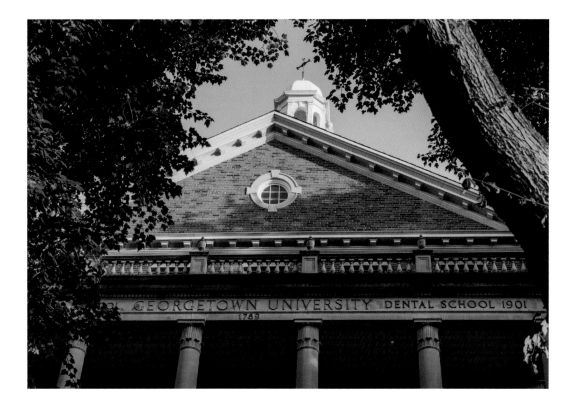

Above: Gustave Doré's illustration of Poe's most famous work, "The Raven." The macabre nature of Poe's own death drew parallels with his dark writing.

Philadelphia because they were against his upcoming union with their sister. The author claims Poe donned a disguise and made his way back to Baltimore to hide from the brothers, but they followed him and beat him some more, forcing whiskey down his throat, which sent him into a state he would never recover from. There is little evidence to back up this theory, however, and it has not been widely supported by Poe experts.

A SICK MAN

If Poe had never traveled to Baltimore, he may well have gone on to marry Shelton and create more celebrated works, although there's plenty of evidence that he was living on borrowed time. In the days before his trip, he'd sought out medical advice because of a fever and a weak pulse. And in July of that year, in a letter to his aunt, Maria Clemm, he had written: "I have been so ill—have had the cholera, or spasms quite as bad, and can now hardly hold the pen." Other illnesses that have been put forward as possible explanations for Poe's delirious state include hypoglycemia, epilepsy, meningitis, brain cancer, and even rabies (see box, opposite). Unfortunately, without an autopsy report, these diagnoses are based largely on reported symptoms and conjecture.

When great artists die, especially under unusual circumstances, people often feel their death should be as unusual as their art. Poe certainly led a life filled with love, loss, darkness, and great writing, but perhaps he really did just succumb to an illness—be it brain cancer, alcoholism, or something else—like an ordinary man. Although that still doesn't explain those bizarre clothes...

— STRANGE —
SUSPICION

Left: A dog infected with rabies. Was Poe's demise caused by the disease?

length of survival for someone infected with rabies after symptoms first show is four days, which fits with Poe's time spent in hospital.

However, Benitez's theory has been widely criticized for relying heavily on the notes of Dr. Moran, whose own opinion on the cause of Poe's death changed some forty years after the fact, and a 1978 article by Charles Scarlett, a prominent businessman and Poe enthusiast, which implies that Poe had difficulty drinking (hydrophobia, an irrational fear of water, is a common symptom of rabies). This is contrary to Dr. Moran's account that Poe drank half a glass of water "without any trouble." Couple with this the fact that Poe had no obvious bite marks and no recollection of being bitten, and it seems unlikely that a rabid animal brought about his death.

In 1996, Dr. Michael Benitez from the University of Maryland Medical Center reviewed Poe's case and found that "the historical accounts of Poe's condition in the hospital a few days before his death point to a strong possibility that he had rabies." He said that in the final stages of the disease, it is common for sufferers to have periods of confusion, changes in pulse rate, and a high temperature, all of which Poe exhibited. And the median

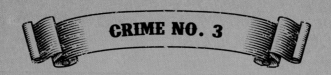

DID LIZZIE BORDEN MURDER HER FATHER AND STEPMOTHER WITH AN AXE?

Date: August 4, 1892
Location: Fall River, Massachusetts, USA

In 1892 a shocking double murder took place in a Massachusetts mill town. The suspect: a well-to-do woman named Lizzie Borden. The victims: her father and stepmother.

Seventy-year-old Andrew Jackson Borden began his career as an undertaker and went on to become president of a bank. He was a relatively wealthy man but lived modestly in a narrow clapboard house in Fall River, Massachusetts, with his second wife, Abby Durfee Gray Borden, and his two grown daughters, Emma and Lizzie. The Bordens also had a live-in maid named Bridget Sullivan.

On the day of the murders, Mrs. Borden was upstairs dusting and Bridget had been cleaning the windows as instructed after vomiting in the yard—the whole household had been ill with the exception of Emma, who was out of town. Mrs. Borden had visited the doctor, worrying their food had been poisoned, but he suspected the sickness was a result of reheating food that was past its best. Bridget chatted with the neighbor's maid over the fence, and headed back inside around the time Mr. Borden arrived home. Bridget heard Lizzie laughing upstairs. Later, exhausted from sickness and her duties, Bridget left Lizzie ironing handkerchiefs in the dining room and Mr. Borden relaxing on the sofa, and retired to her bedroom in the attic.

Ten minutes later, Bridget was summoned by Lizzie yelling: "Come down… Father's dead! Somebody's come in and killed him!" Andrew had been attacked with a small, sharp hatchet, hit ten or eleven times in the face. A commotion followed as Bridget alerted a neighbor and the doctor. That was when Lizzie told her she'd heard Mrs. Borden come home and that she was probably upstairs. Bridget, together with a neighbor, went to check and found Abby lying on the floor of the guest room, similarly mutilated. It's believed she was struck eighteen times with the same weapon. Unlike Mr. Borden, Abby's body was cold. It was estimated she had died some time before her husband.

Below: Lizzie Borden was thirty-two when she was tried for the double murder of her father and stepmother. She denied killing them and was cleared in court, but her reputation as a murderer persists to this day.

ARRESTED FOR MURDER

Lizzie Borden was thirty-two years old when, one week later, she was arrested for the double murder of her father and stepmother. As Lizzie was a Sunday school teacher and an active member of the community, it was shocking news. Borden was unmarried and described by novelist and neighbor Victoria Lincoln as "tall, stocky, jowly, dressy, and unremarkable." No matter her status, it was virtually unheard of for a woman,

Left: The Borden family house still stands at 92 Second Street (now 230) in Fall River. Today it's a Lizzie Borden-themed bed and breakfast.

and a reasonably wealthy woman at that, to be accused of such a violent and intimate crime.

There were a number of elements that led to Lizzie Borden being the prime suspect in the case. The first and most significant to the police was her demeanor. She simply didn't behave how they expected a woman to behave in those circumstances. Officer Harrington noted that: "There was not the least indication of agitation, no sign of sorrow or grief, no lamentation of the heart, no comment on the horror of the crime, and no expression of a wish that the criminal be caught." On top of that was the fact she stood to gain financially from the deaths. While the Bordens didn't live extravagantly, Andrew had accumulated a fortune worth close to $500,000—the equivalent of $10 million today. With Abby dead too, Emma and Lizzie would inherit everything.

Other factors also showed Lizzie in a suspicious light. A drug store clerk claimed Lizzie had visited the pharmacy the day before the murders to purchase prussic acid, otherwise known as hydrogen cyanide, a deadly poison. And the morning after the murders, Lizzie burned a blue dress that she said was stained with paint, but that the prosecutors believed to be stained with blood. The final nail in the coffin was the inquest. Lizzie testified over three days from August 9 to 11. She gave contradictory and incomplete statements, and struggled to provide satisfactory answers. However, the trauma of discovering the body of her father could explain her demeanor.

THE UNKNOWN MAN

During the inquest Lizzie mentioned a man who had come to the house to do business in the fortnight before her father's death. She heard the man say, "I would like to have that store." And her father had refused the man's proposition. "Then they talked a while," Lizzie told the inquest, "and then their voices were louder, and I heard father order him out." Other than this man, whose identity was never discovered, there was no one else for the police to investigate. With nothing taken from the house, the murders appeared to be crimes of passion. The only other potential suspect was John Vinnicum Morse, Andrew's brother-in-law from his first marriage. Morse had stayed at the Bordens' and had been with Andrew in the town's business district that morning. But he had a number of witnesses attesting to his whereabouts at the time the crime was committed. With Bridget sick and resting in her room and Emma out of town, Lizzie looked guiltier than ever.

Below: Lizzie Borden's trial was a national sensation and featured in newspapers and periodicals across the United States.

TRIAL AND ACQUITTAL

She went on trial ten months later. Summing up her defense, her lawyer, A. V. Jennings, declared: "There is not one particle of direct evidence in this case from beginning to end against Lizzie A. Borden. There is not a spot of blood, there is not a weapon that they have connected with her in any way, shape, or fashion." After an hour of deliberating, the jury found her not guilty. The trial had gripped the nation. The *New York Times* wrote: "It will be with a certain relief to every right-minded man or woman who has followed the case that the jury at New Bedford has not only acquitted Miss Lizzie Borden … but has done so with a promptness that was very significant." Despite the evidence, and lack of other potential suspects, the jury could not get on board with the idea that a woman of good-standing could commit such a crime—the state had not hung a woman (the penalty for murder) for centuries.

Above: A courtroom illustration of Lizzie's trial. Her sister, Emma, sits beside her and covers her face.

After Lizzie's acquittal, she and her sister used their inheritance to buy a big house with four bathrooms in the Hill, the town's affluent neighborhood. Eventually Emma moved out, possibly because of her sister's damaged reputation, which never recovered, and Lizzie lived there alone until she died in 1927, aged sixty-seven. Only the undertaker's assistants were present for her interment.

Whether she was wrongfully accused or wrongfully acquitted, Lizzie Borden's name will forever be associated with this vicious crime. She was cleared in court, but for years afterward American children playing in the streets right outside her house and all around the country would sing the rhyme:

Lizzie Borden took an axe
And gave her mother forty whacks
When she saw what she had done
She gave her father forty-one.

— STRANGE —
SUSPICION

If Lizzie did kill her father and stepmother, one theory has been posed in more recent years to make sense of her motive. It focuses on the idea that Lizzie, and possibly her sister too, was a victim of incest at the hands of her father, and that these repressed memories resurfaced, causing her to act out violently. Theorists who support this point to the unusual layout of the Borden house with its two staircases, requiring a person to go up one staircase to the master bedroom and up a separate staircase to the girls' rooms. They think Andrew had the house remodeled in a way that enabled him to abuse his daughters more easily, as Abby would not need to go up the stairs to the girls' rooms to access her own bedroom. Lizzie and Emma's lack of overt sorrow after their father's murder also leads some to think they were both glad to see him dead. During the trial Lizzie's friend Alice Russell testified that Lizzie had come to her the night before and announced that she would soon be taking a vacation. She quoted Lizzie as saying:

Above: Some think Lizzie and Emma's father, Andrew Borden, might have abused his daughters as children.

"something is hanging over me—I cannot tell what it is … I feel afraid something is going to happen." Was this a foretelling of the revenge she was about to inflict on her father?

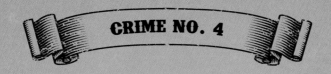

CRIME NO. 4

WHO ASSASSINATED MICHAEL COLLINS?

Date: August 22, 1922
Location: County Cork, Ireland

Michael Collins helped negotiate a treaty for Irish independence, but his revolutionary role may have seen him assassinated by the very IRA compatriots he had previously commanded.

Michael Collins came from a proud farming family. Born in 1890, his home was southwest of Cork, Ireland, and he was raised with strong nationalist values. By the time he reached adulthood, these values had become a way of life for him. At the age of twenty-six he was part of the Irish Easter Rising, where, in 1916, in protest of British rule and to establish an independent Irish Republic, a disorganized Irish nationalist force tried and failed to seize a number of important Dublin buildings. Collins ended up going to prison for his efforts. But to the people he represented, this made him a hero, willing to make sacrifices for the independence cause, and by 1919 he had become commander of the Irish Republican Army (IRA).

Although Collins had been heavily involved in a number of violent operations against British forces during the Irish War of Independence (1919–21), he was a well-respected leader. As a result, he was chosen to be part of a delegation in Westminster, London, to try and establish an Anglo-Irish treaty. This treaty, which was signed by Collins on December 6, 1921, enabled twenty-six of Ireland's thirty-two counties collectively to call themselves the Irish Free State. The counties of the Free State would take control over their own affairs, leaving the remaining six northern counties, which were all more in favor of the union with Britain, with the choice to join the Free State or opt out and remain under British rule. The treaty didn't please everyone, however, particularly the Republic's president, Éamon de Valera, who resigned after the treaty was ratified. And although the treaty passed by a small majority, there

were a number of Republicans who felt its terms, particularly in relation to the division of the country, were not in line with their ideology. They felt that Collins had betrayed them.

Above: Michael Collins passionately addresses a crowd on the streets of Dublin in 1922, the year of his death.

Collins found himself stuck in the middle of a civil war: on one side, the pro-treaty Free State army, and on the other, the anti-treaty Republicans. The British government, eager to resolve the issue, was putting pressure on him to restore order or risk the treaty being abolished altogether. Collins chose the treaty over his IRA compatriots, and backed by ex-British and U.S. soldiers, subjected the anti-treaty supporters to the full force of the Free State army. Eight days of bloody fighting in Dublin, from June 28 to July 5, 1922, saw sixty lives lost, culminating in an IRA surrender. He may have secured the terms of the treaty, but in doing so Collins had essentially signed his own death warrant. He was a man hated by many.

Above: Michael Collins' murder depicted by the Parisian newspaper *Le Petit Journal* on September 3, 1922.

On August 22, 1922, Collins was on his way back to Cork, against the advice of his security team, to show his support for the Free State army, which had recently recaptured the city. They had passed the same way earlier that morning. At 7:15 p.m. his convoy made its way down a country road in Béal na Bláth, close to Collins' place of birth, when a roadblock forced the cars to stop. All of a sudden, gunfire rained down on the cars from the surrounding hills. It was an IRA ambush. Rather than order his men to drive on, Collins grabbed a rifle and began to defend himself, but there was little to be done—they were sitting ducks. He was shot through the head and died at the scene, aged just thirty-one. No other members of the group lost their lives, leading most people to believe the ambush was a planned assassination.

"WE ALL KNEW IT WAS SONNY O'NEILL'S BULLET"

Although the shooter responsible for Collins' death was not officially named, many believe the man who took the fatal shot was Denis "Sonny" O'Neill, a former British Army sniper who had fought in World War One. The dumdum bullets he was using that day, which explode on impact, would explain the gaping wound in Collins' skull. Files released from the Military Service Pensions Collections in 2014 revealed that O'Neill was part of the six-man team that ambushed the convoy, although in his statement he did not say he was the one who shot Collins.

O'Neill's interview before the Army Pensions Board (to determine whether he qualified for a government military pension), thirteen years after the incident, also shows that Collins' assassination almost didn't take place. O'Neill said he "accidentally ran into the Ballinablath [sic] thing, Tom Hales and myself … We heard about the party going through in the morning. They took a wrong turning and went into Newcestown. We went down to look at the position in Ballinblath [sic]. We took up a position there, and held it till late in the evening." In the interview O'Neill was not asked about his involvement with regards to killing Collins. But in the biography *Michael Collins* by Tim Pat Coogan (published 1990) the author mentions that O'Neill was a deeply religious man who was upset and "fundamentally disturbed" by the events of that fateful day. He was aware of shooting a tall officer, whoever that was, before making his getaway. He later told his commanding officer that he thought it was him who had fired the fatal shot. Furthermore, Liam Deasy, the commander of the ambush party, reportedly said: "We all knew it was Sonny O'Neill's bullet."

When Collins signed the treaty in 1921, he had said: "I signed it because I would not be one of those to commit the Irish people

Below: Destruction in the city: the Battle of Dublin lasted for eight days (June 28 to July 5) and included the bombardment of the Four Courts, the home of Ireland's highest courts.

to war without the Irish people committing themselves to war ... I can state for you a principle which everybody will understand, the principle of government by the consent of the governed." But when Collins died, the civil war did not die with him. If anything, the situation got worse. Despite the fact that 500,000 people turned out to see Collins' coffin paraded through the streets of Dublin—one-fifth of the country's population at the time—robberies, vandalism, and more murders continued to be perpetuated by those fighting on both sides of the cause. It wasn't until April 30, 1923, that the IRA admitted defeat and a ceasefire was agreed. While the southern counties finally gained their independence in 1949, the hostility of the civil war was to pervade Irish politics for many years to come.

Below: *Love of Ireland* by Sir John Lavery depicts Michael Collins lying in state. At his funeral, 500,000 people lined the streets to see his coffin parade past.

— STRANGE —
SUSPICION

With all the fingers pointed at the IRA, is there any possibility that Collins was actually killed by someone on his own side? One theory argues that he was shot under the orders of senior government figures who were concerned about Collins' popularity, believing he might become a dictator. However, there's little evidence to support this. In fact, cabinet meeting minutes for that summer show that Collins' opinion was always sought out and major decisions weren't taken without him. Moreover, his colleagues were distraught after his death.

But if an internal conspiracy wasn't to blame, maybe someone in the convoy had a change of heart and switched sides. A few months after Collins' death, on December 2, John McPeake, the armored car machine gunner whose gun had jammed that night while protecting Collins, deserted to the Republican side. He reportedly told a female friend that he was looking to get out of the National Army as he was being treated badly by

Above: National Army soldiers during the Irish Civil War, which continued after Collins' shocking death.

his fellow soldiers because of the gun jam. The IRA arranged to help with his desertion, as long as he stole the Slievenamon (the armored car). He was caught and spent six years in prison for the theft. Theorists believe McPeake may have deserted sooner, working for the IRA from the inside. This belief is fueled by the rumor that when de Valera later regained power, McPeake may have received a Secret Service pension—a reward for keeping his mouth shut about what really happened that night or a pat on the back for his attempted desertion.

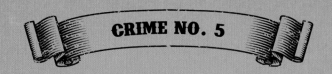

WAS AL CAPONE BEHIND THE ST. VALENTINE'S DAY MASSACRE?

Date: February 14, 1929
Location: Chicago, Illinois, USA

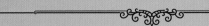

Valentine's Day in Chicago will forever be tarnished by what the *New York Times* described as "the most cold-blooded gang massacre in the history of this city's underworld."

On a cold February morning in 1929, a group of known gangsters were gathered in a garage at 2122 North Clark Street, Chicago. It was Valentine's Day, but they weren't there to exchange cards and flowers; this was a business meeting between seven of George "Bugs" Moran's men. Moran was one of Al Capone's biggest rivals, and the two vied for control over the city's smuggling and trafficking operations during prohibition. Dressed in fine suits and ties, the group looked dapper. Each man carried a few thousand dollars in cash to pay for a shipment of illegal booze they'd been told would be delivered that morning. But this was no run-of-the-mill delivery. They were expecting to meet with their boss and two of his associates. Unfortunately for them, it wasn't to be. Unknowingly, the men had gotten dressed for the last time.

Above: Cook County Coroner Dr. Bundesen (gray suit) presides over a police reenactment of the massacre.

At 10:30 a.m. four or five (this point is still debated) other men walked into the garage. Two were dressed in police uniforms. Despite being armed, Moran's men didn't reach for their weapons. They were accustomed to dealings with the police, so perhaps they thought the cops were carrying out a search. Raising their weapons—two Tommy guns and two 12-gauge shotguns—the newcomers ordered the gangsters to stand shoulder to shoulder, facing the garage's north wall, as if they were about to make arrests. Then they opened fire, spraying the bodies with bullets. Most of the men died instantly. By the time the perpetrators were through, over a hundred machine gun shells had been emptied onto the garage floor. The bodies were a bloody mess and the wall was riddled with sinew and bullet holes.

Frank Gusenberg was the last to die, at 1:35 p.m. He'd been taken to Alexian Brothers Hospital, but had lost a lot of blood and was too weak for surgery. Just before he died a police sergeant repeatedly asked him who was responsible. He reportedly replied, "No one shot me." Gusenberg, whose brother Pete was also among the dead, was abiding by the code of the underworld, by refusing to snitch, even with his dying breath. The Gusenbergs had recently failed to assassinate Jack McGurn, one of Al Capone's top men, who many believe to be responsible for orchestrating the Valentine's Day attack. The five other men left for dead inside the garage were Moran's brother-in-law and bank robber Albert Kachellek, aka James Clark; Moran's business manager, Adam Heyer; saloon keeper Albert Weinshank; the gang's mechanic, John May; and optometrist and bootlegging associate, Dr. Reinhart Schwimmer.

One man who avoided injury altogether was Moran. He was living at the nearby Parkway Hotel and was on his way to the garage when the shooting took place. It's believed that Moran was actually the primary target, but that the killers' lookout mistook one of the other seven men for him, causing the shooters to arrive too early. Nine days after the massacre, Cook County's coroner, Dr. Herman Bundesen, held an inquest into the deaths. Each man was shot at least fifteen times, mostly in the back or the head. Some of them had also been shot while they lay dying on the ground.

WHO WERE THE SHOOTERS?

Despite numerous witnesses seeing men coming and going from the garage, no one has ever been convicted of the massacre.

Below: Five of the seven victims of the shooting, as their bodies were found by police.

Right: George Moran's rival, Al Capone. Capone was in Miami, Florida, at the time of the shooting but might have masterminded it from afar.

However, two men were charged with the crime: Jack "Machine Gun" McGurn and John Scalise, two of Al Capone's most trusted men. Both were later released due to lack of evidence. A number of other potential shooters have also been named, including Capone's men Albert Anselmi and Byron Bolton, and some evidence points to the fact that two of the shooters might have been from out of town. A manuscript written by Georgette Winkler, the wife of St. Louis mobster Gus Winkler, recounts how the couple moved to Chicago in 1927 along with Fred "Killer" Burke, and that on the morning of the massacre the two men were dressed in police uniforms, something they frequently used as a tactic in robberies.

Two years later, Burke was convicted of the murder of a Michigan police officer in an unrelated case. A leading ballistics expert studied the evidence from that case and found that the bullets and shells that had been used matched those found in the Valentine's Day victims' bodies—the same gun (and probably the same shooter) had been present at both crimes. Burke was sent to prison for life for murder, but was never charged in relation to the Chicago massacre.

THE BLONDE ALIBI

Despite eyewitnesses placing him at the scene, Al Capone's chief bodyguard and hitman Jack McGurn got off, in large part because he had one of the most famous alibis of the twentieth century. The "Blonde Alibi," as she soon became known, was McGurn's girlfriend Louisa Rolfe. McGurn told police that he and Rolfe didn't leave their suite at the lavish Stevens Hotel from 9 p.m. on February 13 until 3 p.m. the day of the murders. He even signed his real name on the register, "Vincent Gebaldi," to strengthen his alibi. And while police had enough evidence to disprove it, in 1931 McGurn married Rolfe, enabling him to invoke "spousal privilege" in court, which would prevent Rolfe from being forced to testify, and the charges against him were dropped.

WHERE WAS CAPONE?

Al Capone was a known rival of Moran's, and when the latter was tracked down in the days after the massacre, he reportedly said, "Only Capone kills like that." With the finger pointed at him, the cops descended on his Lexington Hotel suite and his home at 7244 Prairie Avenue, but he wasn't there: Capone had been staying in Miami, Florida, over 1,000 miles away. Police checked his phone records, and there were no calls to Chicago made in the days just before or after the massacre. This was unusual—he normally placed calls to Chicago every day—but it made it hard for police to connect Capone with the killings. He even had a solid alibi for the exact time the shootings took place: he was having a meeting with the Dade County solicitor.

Although the police never could pin the 1929 shootings on McGurn or Capone, the careers of both men dried up shortly after. Just after the clock struck midnight, seven years to the day after the massacre, McGurn was murdered in a bowling alley by three armed assailants, shot in the back of the head. By that time Capone was already in prison serving a six-and-a-half-year sentence for tax evasion. He was later released and died in 1947.

STRANGE
SUSPICION

Left: The spates of gangland killings in 1920s Chicago had a lot to do with the illegal booze trade during Prohibition.

One of the most shocking elements of the case was the fact that the killers were dressed as police officers and used detective-style cars to make their getaway. The disguise was a great tactic, causing confusion for witnesses, and it meant that the Chicago Police Department had to first rule out their own colleagues. There were undoubtedly lots of honest cops on the beat, but the suspicions were reasonable. Gang members routinely paid off police to turn a blind eye to their activities, and given the ferocity of the city's gang violence, it was inevitable that armed police would, on occasion, be involved in deadly shootings. In fact, less than two years earlier, a Chicago police officer had shot and killed a previous gang leader named Vincent "Schemer" Drucci while he was unarmed and in police custody. When McGurn was being questioned the police asked him who he thought was responsible for the Valentine's Day shootings: "Aw, a squad of cops, probably," he said. "They probably had been doing business with Moran and found things getting hot and had to bump 'em all off."

The Cook County State Attorney's Office began its own investigation into the murders, in case any police were involved, but found no evidence against the force. On top of that, coroner Dr. Bundesen empaneled a special jury to examine the case to avoid any claims of corruption. These inquiries showed the high levels of mistrust in law enforcement, and probably only served to hinder the investigation.

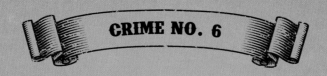

CRIME NO. 6

WHO KILLED SIR HARRY OAKES?

Date: July 8, 1943
Location: Nassau, Bahamas

With a murdered millionaire, royal connections, and an exotic island location, the tale of Sir Harry Oakes' death reads like a classic detective story, with one exception: it's true.

Sir Harry Oakes was a Bahamian multimillionaire, originally from Maine, in the USA, who'd made his fortune through Canadian gold mining. He was lured to the tax haven of Nassau in the Bahamas by his friend and business partner, Harold Christie, and had lived there for nine years. But Oakes' lavish life on the "Isles of June" was cut short when someone decided to bring about his premature death.

At 7 a.m. on Thursday, July 8, 1943, Christie, who'd been staying at Oakes' house, walked into his friend's bedroom to find the sixty-nine-year-old dead in his bed. His head had been struck with a spiked object, crushing his skull. The murderer had then doused the body in petrol, covered it with pillow feathers, and set it alight. An electric fan had been placed at the foot of the bed to fan the flames. The fire's obvious goal was to destroy any evidence of Oakes' murder and make his death appear to be a tragic accident.

However, the weather had other plans, and a heavy storm that night soon put the flames out. When Oakes was discovered, the pajamas on one side of his body had burned away and his skin was covered in heat blisters. This was no accident. Someone had brutally attacked the millionaire and vanished—but not without a trace. There were bloody handprints all over the walls and a Chinese screen, and the stairs were covered in muddy footprints heading in the direction of Christie's bedroom.

Above: Sir Harry Oakes photographed in 1941, two years before the multimillionaire's death.

"A RIDICULOUS CHARGE"

As word spread of this high-society horror, everyone was wondering who would want to bump off one of the island's biggest benefactors? His business interests provided jobs for locals and he had set up a number of community outreach projects. When rich people are killed, usually it is those who stand to gain financially who are considered likely suspects. So locals were immediately suspicious of Alfred de Marigny, a Mauritian with a French title who was married to Oakes' daughter, Nancy. The next day detectives questioned Marigny at Oakes' house. Less than thirty-six hours after the discovery of the body, Marigny was in a cell, charged with the murder of his father-in-law. In a statement he issued voluntarily, Marigny said: "It is a ridiculous charge."

Initially, the strongest piece of evidence against Marigny was a single fingerprint found on the Chinese screen in Oakes' room. But under cross-examination in court, it became obvious that the detectives had planted it there to implicate Marigny. The prime

suspect had spent most of the night at his own home hosting a dinner party. He had driven a few guests home, driving past Oakes' home, leaving only thirty minutes of his evening for which he had no alibi. Marigny's trial was big news in the United States and the UK—it even forced World War Two off the front pages— as was his acquittal.

One person who escaped with his reputation intact was Oakes' friend Christie, the man who'd discovered the body. No one thought it was unusual that he had slept through the whole murder or that his claim of spending the night at Oakes' home was disputed by locals who had seen him in town. Add to this the fact that Christie owed Oakes money, and there were enough red flags to warrant bringing him in for questioning. But, whether because of his social standing or the assumption of Marigny's guilt, Christie was never formally considered a suspect in the case. If he did know the truth, it died with him in 1973, when he passed away a very wealthy man.

Above: The murder scene at Harry Oakes' house shows the burned and bloodied bed clothes; the screen where Marigny's fingerprint was found stands beside the bed.

— STRANGE —
SUSPICION

A surprisingly high-profile individual took a personal interest in the Oakes murder investigation. The Duke of Windsor (formerly King Edward VIII, before his abdication) had been granted the title of Governor of the Bahamas in 1940. He had known Oakes well and used his position of power to overrule the Bahamian criminal investigation department, bringing in two detectives from Miami to take charge of the case. These two officers, Captains James Barker and Edward Melchen, arrived in the Bahamas on Thursday afternoon without the proper equipment to photograph fingerprints and postponed their search until the next day. They made no attempt to locate a murder weapon and did not take precautions to secure the crime scene, allowing visitors and reporters into the house. After the duke's Friday visit, where he spoke with them privately for half an hour, the detectives charged Marigny and then instructed the local police to scrub the walls of the bedroom, removing any evidence of other prints.

Above: The Duke of Windsor, formerly King Edward VIII of the United Kingdom, was heavily involved in the investigation into Oakes' murder.

During Marigny's interrogation on that Friday afternoon, he was offered an unopened packet of Lucky Strike cigarettes. It's believed this was how the police obtained a print to plant at the crime scene. Some theories suggest that the duke had borrowed a large sum of money from the millionaire or that his wife was having an affair with him, and the cover-up was to avoid these salacious details being made public. But it's more likely that the former king wanted to see the whole mess put to bed as quickly as possible, even if it meant an innocent man going to the gallows.

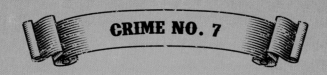

WHO WAS RESPONSIBLE FOR THE BLACK DAHLIA MURDER?

Date: January 15, 1947
Location: Los Angeles, California, USA

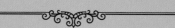

Her body was discovered mutilated beyond measure; her killer was never found. Her name was Elizabeth Short, but she's better known as the Black Dahlia.

Elizabeth Short was born in Massachusetts and was twenty-two years old at the time of her death. Her family called her Betty. As a teenager she'd spent time in Florida working as a cinema usherette and doing some part-time modeling. As a young adult, she traveled a lot, living in Miami, Atlanta, Boston, and California—she wanted to be a movie star and Los Angeles was the place to be seen.

The last time anyone reported seeing Short alive was on January 9, 1947, when she'd been waiting at the Biltmore Hotel in downtown Los Angeles. After depositing her luggage at the Greyhound bus station, as she had plans to travel onward to Boston, she'd been dropped off at the Biltmore, supposedly to rendezvous with her sister. Hotel employees reported seeing her making a number of phone calls from the hotel lobby before she left, heading toward Sixth Street.

A BROKEN MANNEQUIN

At 10 a.m. on January 15, housewife and mother Betty Bersinger was pushing her three-year-old daughter in a stroller on her way to get some shoes repaired. As they made their way down Norton Avenue, in the Oakwood neighborhood of LA, she noticed something white on the verge, close to the edge of the sidewalk. Her initial thought was that it was a store mannequin—its legs detached from the torso, its arms raised above its head—until she moved a little closer. Bersinger was staring at the corpse of Elizabeth Short.

Short's killer had performed a hemicorporectomy on her body. This procedure, where the lower body is amputated below the waist, was developed as a way of saving soldiers who had suffered combat trauma during the two World Wars. Short's body had been severed beneath the lumbar spine—the only place it can be cut in half

Below: After she was murdered in Los Angeles in 1947, Elizabeth Short became better known by her nickname, the Black Dahlia.

without breaking any bones. In 1949, in his sworn testimony before the Los Angeles County Grand Jury, Detective Harry Hansen told the court that he had a theory as to what type of person had killed Short. "I think that a medical man committed the murder, a fine surgeon," he said. "I base that conclusion on the way the body was bisected … It is unusual in this sense, that the point at which the body was bisected is, according to eminent medical men, the easiest spot in the spinal column to sever … He hit it exactly." Hansen went on to explain that he had seen many mutilated bodies during his time in the Los Angeles Police Department (LAPD), but this case was noticeably different.

Among other horrific acts involving feces and her own pubic hair, Short's face had also been mutilated with a long gash extending each side of her mouth to create an eerie smile. Later examination of her body revealed that her uterus and intestines had been removed, before her death. There were rope marks on her wrists, ankles, and around her neck. Remarkably, there was no blood. Short's body had been completely drained and her skin was described as being "white as a lily."

THE BLACK DAHLIA

Gruesome and grisly murders like that of Elizabeth Short sell newspapers, and this was especially true in the 1940s, when journalists were often able to photograph corpses and gain access to crime scenes. Not long after the police arrived at Norton Avenue, hotshot reporter Agness "Aggie" Underwood of the *Herald-Express* showed up too. It is Underwood who is most often credited with the nickname attributed to Short's murder.

Below: An advertisement seeking information about Short's whereabouts in the days leading up to her death.

Vol. 40 Tuesday, January 21, 1947 No. 14

WANTED INFORMATION ON ELIZABETH SHORT
Between Dates January 9 and 15, 1947

Description: Female, American, 22 years, 5 ft. 6 in., 118 lbs., black hair, green eyes, very attractive, bad lower teeth, finger nails chewed to quick. This subject found brutally murdered, body severed and mutilated January 15, 1947, at 39th and Norton.

Subject on whom information wanted last seen January 9, 1947 when she got out of car at Biltmore Hotel. At that time she was wearing black suit, no collar on coat, probably Cardigan style, white fluffy blouse, black suede high-heeled shoes, nylon stockings, white gloves full-length beige coat, carried black plastic handbag (2 handles) 12 x 8. in which she had black address book. Subject readily makes friends with both sexes and frequented cocktail bars and night spots. On leaving car she went into lobby of the Biltmore, and was last seen there.

Inquiry should be made at all hotels, motels, apartment houses, cocktail bars and lounges, night clubs to ascertain whereabouts of victim between dates mentioned. In conversations subject readily identified herself as Elizabeth or "Beth" Short.

Attention Officers H. H. Hansen and F. A. Brown, Homicide Detail.

KINDLY NOTIFY C. B. HORRALL, CHIEF OF POLICE, LOS ANGELES, CALIFORNIA.

It wasn't uncommon for killers or their victims to be named in this way by newspaper journalists—it made for punchy headlines. There were other women victims whose murders were associated with flowers, including the Red Hibiscus murder and the White Gardenia murder. Short's killing was originally referred to as the Werewolf Murder, as were a number of other murders of women at this time, but the later name, and the one that would stick, was derived from the 1946 Veronica Lake film noir *The Blue Dahlia*. "Black" was a reference to Short's striking hair color.

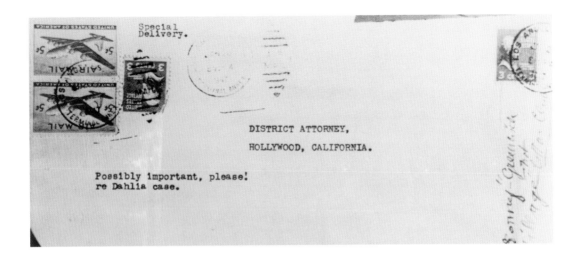

The police and the press had a cozy relationship in post-war California. And this access and sharing of information could prove both fruitful and detrimental to a case. While traveling and working as a waitress in Los Angeles, Short had had a number of male companions. This, combined with the publicity surrounding her death, meant there were multiple suspects and hundreds of people who, seeking the notoriety, came forward claiming to have killed her. The body had been cleaned thoroughly, however, leaving no real physical evidence to connect anyone to the case, and there were no witnesses to the killing.

It is possible that Short's killer was someone known to her—a date gone sour, perhaps—but it was equally likely she had been picked up by a friendly stranger while hitchhiking (a common practice back then), her fate sealed as she got into the car. One of the first suspects was an army corporal who said he had been with Short in San Francisco a few days before her body was discovered, and had then blacked out. He thought he had committed the murder, but it transpired he had been at his military base the day Short died. The police investigation rumbled on until the news grew tired of it. Then a package addressed to the *Los Angeles Examiner* was picked up from the Biltmore Hotel. Inside, a message read:

Above: This letter, which was smeared with lipstick, was one of a number of leads in the case, although the police never disclosed the letter's contents.

BILTMORE HOTEL, LOS ANGELES, CALIFORNIA   63774 T105

Above: Elizabeth Short was last seen alive at the Biltmore Hotel in Los Angeles, California. The hotel now serves a cocktail named after her.

"Here is Dahlia's belongings." The package also contained an address book, Short's birth certificate, her social security card, and the stubs for the bags she had left at the Greyhound bus station. But all the evidence had been soaked in gasoline to remove fingerprints, and it led to nothing. The killer wanted to be in the headlines, but not for getting caught.

The Black Dahlia case remains open to this day. Elizabeth Short never made it as a movie star, but her name has lived on long after many of the stars of her day, serving as a warning to young women enticed to Hollywood to fulfill their dreams. There is even a cocktail named after her at the Biltmore Hotel—it's a bitter-tasting mix of vodka, Kahlua, and Chambord black raspberry liqueur.

— STRANGE —
SUSPICION

Above: After the death of American physician George Hodel, his son started to suspect him of Short's murder.

In 2000, a former LAPD detective, Steve Hodel, started investigating the murder after finding some photographs among his deceased father's possessions of a woman that closely resembled Short. He believed that his father, a physician named George Hodel, may have been the killer. Steve pieced together anecdotal evidence of conversations between witnesses' family members that implicated a doctor "who lived on Franklin Avenue," where his father had lived at the time of the murder. A handwriting expert said there was a strong chance George's handwriting matched the script in the notes the killer had sent. Steve later sent his research to the district attorney's office. After reviewing the file, Assistant DA Steven Kay wrote back saying that if George were still alive, he would be facing two charges of murder against him.

Steve published his theory in a book that went on to be a bestseller. A journalist writing about the book for the *Los Angeles Times* was sent a file from the DA's office containing notes and interviews taken by Lt. Frank Jemison, one of the case's original officers. The file revealed that there were six prime suspects in the investigation, and one of them was George Hodel. His home was even bugged, and in one 1950 phone call a transcript records George as saying: "Supposin' I did kill the Black Dahlia. They couldn't prove it now. They can't talk to my secretary any more because she's dead."

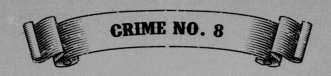

WHO WAS BEHIND THE ASSASSINATION OF ARCHBISHOP OSCAR ROMERO?

Date: March 24, 1980
Location: San Salvador, El Salvador

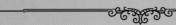

Archbishop Romero had a target on his back, but not even his politically motivated killers could have predicted that a twelve-year civil war would be sparked by his assassination.

In 1977, when Oscar Romero became Archbishop of San Salvador, El Salvador's capital, the country was on the verge of civil war. Left-wing guerilla groups, tired of the feudalistic system and treatment of the peasant farmers, or *campesinos*, had hit back against big business and the military. Backed by U.S. funds, the army and its "death squads" were trying to crush the uprising by any means necessary.

But Romero was not prepared to remain silent. He frequently and publicly denounced the violence on both sides. This earned him his first death threat from the president, Colonel Arturo Molina, who warned the archbishop that "cassocks are not bulletproof." Each Sunday Romero's sermon was broadcast on the radio, and men and women across the country tuned in to hear what he would say next. On March 23, the day before his death, Romero implored the armed forces: "Before any order given by a man, the law of God must prevail: 'You shall not kill!'" He knew he was a likely target for the many people whose actions he was defying; just two weeks before, explosives had been found in a briefcase near a pulpit he was due to preach from.

The next evening, at around 6:30 p.m., Romero was addressing the congregation in the chapel at Divina Providencia Hospital. It was a hot day and the doors to the chapel were open to let the breeze in. He was delivering the homily when a red VW Passat pulled up outside. From the back seat, a tall, thin, bearded man raised an assault rifle and fired. The bullet traveled a distance of 115 feet and struck the archbishop in the heart. He fell to the floor and bled out, his blood staining the white Communion wafers.

Above: Archbishop Oscar Romero captured in one of many wall murals that celebrate his life and work.

OPERATION PINEAPPLE

On May 7, a farm just outside the capital was raided by the military and more than twenty people were arrested. Among them was Major Roberto D'Aubuisson, who many believe was the "intellectual author" of the assassination. In the raid, a significant number of weapons and documents were seized that implicated the group in the organization and financing of the death squads, and Romero's murder. In particular, these included Captain Álvaro Rafael Saravia's operational notebook and a piece of paper belonging to D'Aubuisson that contained details of an assignment dubbed "Operation Pineapple," widely believed to be the code name for Romero's assassination. It included a list of the components needed to carry out the operation, including a driver,

Above: During the civil war, left-wing guerrilla groups began to fight back in rural Salvadoran communities, frustrated by the treatment of peasant farmers.

a four-strong security detail, and a sniper. The driver, named Amado Garay, was thought to be organized by Captain Saravia. The sniper was believed to be a former national guardsman called Oscar Perez Linares, who was paid $200 to take the shot.

Despite all this evidence against D'Aubuisson and others, terrorist threats and institutional pressure resulted in their release from arrest. No further charges were brought. D'Aubuisson left the military shortly after Romero's assassination but didn't shy away from the spotlight. He became one of the country's leading politicians. In 1984 he was narrowly defeated in his bid for the presidency, but his party, ARENA, went from strength to strength.

In 2003 the Center for Justice and Accountability (CJA) in San Francisco filed a civil lawsuit against Saravia, who was living in the United States at the time. Saravia, who remains on U.S. Immigration's most-wanted list, never responded to the court order and went into hiding.

No one has ever stood trial in El Salvador for the death of Oscar Romero. Not long after the Chapultepec Peace Accords were signed in 1992, a blanket amnesty law was passed by the Salvadoran Legislative Assembly, which was dominated by D'Aubuisson's ARENA party. The law prevented investigation into the human rights violations and crimes committed during the civil war period. In 2016 the law was overturned by the Salvadoran Supreme Court and declared "contrary to the access

— STRANGE —
SUSPICION

Some people think the professional nature of Romero's assassination must have been the work of the CIA. Although it's now widely accepted that a national guardsman team was responsible for the hit, there is evidence that U.S. President Ronald Reagan's administration knew much more than it publicly disclosed about the human rights abuses being perpetrated in El Salvador. Romero had written a letter to Reagan's predecessor, Jimmy Carter, urging him not to intervene by sending military support, knowing it would be used to prop up the death squads. The archbishop was assassinated a month later. A week after his death, the U.S. approved a budget of $5.7 million in emergency military aid to prevent the spread of Soviet Communism in Central America. During the Reagan years, U.S. embassy officials handed over evidence to the CIA that implicated

Above: President Ronald Reagan's administration was heavily invested in preventing the spread of Communism in South America.

D'Aubuisson—who was considered a Cold War ally—in Romero's assassination. But this was kept buried so that Congress would continue to approve sending military aid to the El Salvadoran government.

of justice." In a UN-approved report compiled by the Truth Commission for El Salvador, it was found that D'Aubuisson had ordered Romero's killing.

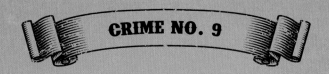

WHO MURDERED THE ITALIAN BANKER ROBERTO CALVI?

Date: June 18, 1982
Location: London, UK

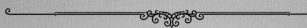

Roberto Calvi's name will forever be associated with dodgy banking, Mafia murder, and corruption at the highest levels of the Catholic Church.

It was a shocking sight for London's early risers making their way to work one June morning in 1982. The time was 7:30 a.m. when a postal clerk first spotted an orange rope hanging from a pipe under the northernmost arch of Blackfriars Bridge. A man was hanging from the rope by his neck and the water was lapping at his feet. Thirty minutes later, the police arrived to inspect the corpse. The man appeared to be in his sixties and had dyed black hair. He was dressed in an expensive suit and was wearing a gold watch. But something was amiss—his body appeared bulky and misshapen. After cutting him down police found the cause: 12 pounds' worth of stones and bricks were stuffed into his clothing. His pockets also contained a fake passport; $13,700 in British, Italian, and Swiss currency; a pocket watch; and two wallets.

The body, police soon discovered, belonged to a wealthy Italian banker named Roberto Calvi. He was wanted in Italy, where a judge had issued a fugitive warrant for his arrest. Calvi had been convicted of criminal fraud crimes and sentenced to four years in prison. He had fled the country while on bail awaiting his appeal. Suicide by hanging was an obvious conclusion to draw. After all, Calvi was a man on the run; he had attempted suicide before, slashing his wrists and taking an overdose while in custody in Italy; his watch and money had not been taken; there were no marks on his body to suggest a struggle or a fight in the lead-up to his death; and the toxicology report showed no signs of drugs, with the exception of a sleeping pill taken the night before.

The first inquest into Calvi's death found that he had died by suicide—although the jury was not unanimous. The second, which took place a year later at the request of Calvi's family, returned an open verdict. And it's not hard to see why. There were a number of factors that didn't add up. For starters, if Calvi was planning to kill himself, why make the trip to London at all? Why not just kill himself in Rome? The distance between Calvi's accommodation in West London and Blackfriars Bridge was at least four and a half miles. His journey would have taken him past many other Thames crossings before reaching Blackfriars, so why pick this particular bridge to carry out a public suicide?

Below: Roberto Calvi, who became known as "God's Banker" because of his ties to the Catholic Church.

The bricks in Calvi's pockets also posed a problem for the theory that the Italian's death was of his own making. Police matched the stones on his person to a building site some

Above: Calvi's compatriots, Flavio Carboni (left) and Silvano Vittor, on trial in Rome in 2005.

985 feet away from where he died. If Calvi had collected and carried the stones himself, there would've been trace residue on his hands, but the coroner found none. There was also the question of how an unfit middle-aged man with vertigo managed to get to the hanging spot unaided. It would have required a degree of athleticism that he didn't possess. This, combined with the fact that no rust from the bridge's 25-foot ladder was found on his suit, hands, or shoes, pointed to foul play.

ON THE RUN

Calvi was a man living in fear. He'd spent just three days in London prior to his death. It had taken him a week to get to the British capital, flying from Rome to Venice, and driving to Trieste, before catching a fishing trawler to Muggia, an Italian town on the border with Yugoslavia. From there he was smuggled into Austria, where he posed as an executive for Fiat and used his fake passport to board a private charter flight to London. Calvi's reason for visiting the city has never come to light.

Once he'd arrived, Calvi didn't check into a luxury hotel. Instead, he was holed up in a pokey room at the Chelsea Cloisters guesthouse in South Kensington, paying just £40 ($50) a night. He reportedly spent most of his time in his room using the telephone and hardly left the building. He'd also shaved off his moustache, which many believe to have been an attempt to hide his identity. Calvi reportedly called his daughter, worried about his situation, and told his wife Clara: "I don't trust the people I'm with anymore." He had traveled to London with two men, a cigarette smuggler named Silvano Vittor and Sardinian businessman Flavio

Carboni, both of whom had connections to the Mafia. Somewhat suspiciously, they both returned to Italy immediately after his death, so police were unable to question them. It was later discovered that Carboni took Calvi's briefcase with him. It was believed to be filled with important documents pertaining to the banker's fraudulent dealings.

WHO WANTED CALVI DEAD?

Roberto Calvi wasn't any ordinary banker. In fact, when he died, he wasn't a banker at all. He had been fired from his role at Banco Ambrosiano the day before. The private bank, where he had been chairman and managing director, would collapse shortly after his death, having amassed debts of $1.4 billion. Under Calvi's chairmanship, Banco Ambrosiano laundered money for the Sicilian Mafia's heroin dealings, some of which Calvi was accused of stealing. When the Bank of Italy investigated, they found that huge sums of money had "disappeared" into illegal offshore accounts. Calvi also regularly handled large financial payments made by companies to Italy's political parties. There were many people

Below: Calvi's body was found hanging from Blackfriars Bridge in London, England.

who stood to lose, financially and personally, from the bank's imminent demise. Calvi's only remaining card was his knowledge and documents he possessed relating to other people's misdeeds. Many people, including Calvi's family, believed he was killed so that these secrets would be buried with him.

In 1991, Mafia godfather Francesco "Frankie the Strangler" Di Carlo was named as Calvi's killer by a supergrass, although he was never arrested. Eleven years later, Di Carlo told a journalist how two days before Calvi's death, Pippo Calò, known as "the Mafia's cashier," had tried to contact him about carrying out the hit, but that the job was done by someone else. He did, however, explain that the Mafia wanted Calvi dead: "No one had any trust in him anymore," said Di Carlo. "He owed a lot of money … Everyone wanted to get rid of him."

More than twenty-three years after his body was found in London, in 2005 five people stood trial in a Rome court for Roberto Calvi's murder. The prosecutors alleged that Pippo Calò had ordered Calvi's killing and that Carboni and Vittor had accompanied him to London to deliver him into the hands of his killer. Also on trial were Carboni's ex-girlfriend, Manuela Kleinszig, and businessman Ernesto Diotallevi. They all had ties to the Mafia. After a trial lasting a year and a half, all five defendants were acquitted. The true story of the banker and Blackfriars Bridge remains a mystery … for now.

Below: The northernmost archway of Blackfriars Bridge, where its believed a hitman, possibly Francesco Di Carlo, hung Calvi's body.

— STRANGE —
SUSPICION

The banking revelations were also embarrassing for the Catholic Church. Calvi was trusted by the Institute for the Works of Religion—the Vatican's bank—which was the largest shareholder in Ambrosiano. After his death, Calvi earned the nickname "God's Banker." He knew many of the Vatican's darkest financial secrets relating to Mafia connections, and offshore companies and accounts. Just days before his death, Calvi wrote a personal letter to Pope John Paul II, pleading for a meeting with him so he could explain himself. He also claimed to have important documents to show him, and these are believed to have been in the briefcase that Carboni stole.

Through his financial dealings, Calvi also had close ties to the right-wing masonic organization P2. Licio Gelli, the lodge's Grand Master, was later sentenced to twelve years for fraud in connection with the collapse of Ambroisiano. The lodge's membership included many of Italy's leading

Above: Pope John Paul II received a personal letter from Calvi asking for a meeting not long before the banker's death.

political, business, and intelligence figures. The haste and carelessness with which the police carried out their original investigation, particularly by omitting to take crime scene photographs, has led some to think that there was a powerful religious or masonic influence involved, making sure no one looked too closely into Calvi's and the bank's affairs.

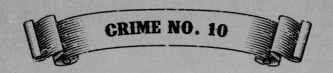

WHO KILLED SWEDISH PRIME MINISTER OLOF PALME?

Date: February 28, 1986
Location: Stockholm, Sweden

Like the dramatic assassination of JFK in the U.S. in 1963, this killing of a political leader, and the subsequent investigation, shocked a country to its core.

Sweden's prime minister, Olof Palme, had been out at the cinema in Stockholm with his wife, Lisbet, his son, and his son's partner to see the comedy *Bröderna Mozart*. It had been a last-minute arrangement, so the Social Democrat was without his bodyguard. The family watched the movie, and then the couples went their separate ways. At 11:21 p.m. on that wintry night, Palme and his wife were walking along the busy thoroughfare Sveavägen, about to make their way into a subway station, when two shots rang out. The Swedish leader had been hit in the back. The assailant fired again, shooting at Lisbet. The prime minister died within minutes, as his killer ran off into the night.

Lisbet, whose injuries weren't fatal, had stood just a few feet from her husband's killer, but she hadn't seen much with which

Right: Olof Palme addressing the crowd at a Swedish Social Democratic party rally. Palme was a divisive politician both at home in Sweden and internationally.

to identify him. There were a number of other witnesses, but the description was very vague: white male, thirty to fifty years old, average height and build. He was wearing a dark coat and his features were obscured by a cap covering much of his face. Very little physical evidence was retrieved by police from the crime scene, and despite the shooting taking place in a busy area of the country's capital city, the killer was able to flee the scene. The .357-caliber Magnum pistol used to fire the shots was never found. The initial police response has been largely blamed for the fact that, after thirty years, the assassin is still on the loose. In the many years since, huge amounts of money have been spent trying to identify the killer, but to no avail.

That's not to say no one has served time for Palme's death. Nearly two years after the shooting, police finally arrested Gustav Christer Pettersson. Forty-two-year-old Pettersson was a drug addict and petty criminal with a previous manslaughter conviction, and he had spent much of his adult life in and out of the prison system. He was convicted largely due to the fact that Lisbet Palme had

Above: Gustav Christer Pettersson was arrested for Palme's murder despite the fact that he had no motive and police had no evidence connecting him to the crime.

picked him out in a lineup. However, there was no physical evidence connecting him to the crime scene. He had no motive to want Palme dead (in fact he was a fellow socialist) or to kill him in such a risky manner, and the investigation into him did not result in police finding the murder weapon. Nevertheless, at trial in 1988, a jury found him guilty of the assassination. Nearly a year after he was sentenced, however, an appeal court found that Mrs. Palme's identification of him as the killer, so long after the fact, was not enough evidence for a conviction. Pettersson was released with $50,000 in compensation for his time spent in prison. He died of a blow to the head from a fall in 2004.

A POLITICAL ATTACK

There have been other suspects. The first man to have the finger of blame pointed firmly at him, long before Petersson was charged with the crime, was Viktor Gunnarsson, a Swedish extremist and member of a number of right-wing groups, who detested Palme's politics. On the night of the assassination he had been seen at a restaurant and cinema not far from the murder scene, and had been spotted in a McDonald's close by at 1:10 a.m. On top of that, a taxi driver who identified Gunnarsson in a lineup said he had picked up a man not far from the murder scene who got into the cab yelling, "Drive me anywhere—I will pay you anything you want!" It later transpired that the taxi driver, who spoke very little Swedish, had been coached by police beforehand, and had initially selected different men in the lineup. There was no concrete evidence to

Right: Abdullah Ocalan, one of the founding members of the Kurdish Workers' Party, claimed that Palme's murder was carried out by Kurdish terrorists.

hold Gunnarsson and he was later released without charge. During the course of the investigation 134 people claimed that they had killed Palme. And as tends to happen with politically motivated crimes, a number of groups came out of the woodwork to claim the atrocity for their cause. One such group was the Kurdish Workers' Party. In 2001, while being interviewed in prison by Swedish investigators, Kurdish rebel leader Abdullah Ocalan claimed that a dissident Kurdish group had assassinated the prime minister. In the 1980s, a number of Kurdish terrorists had taken sanctuary in Sweden, but Sweden had extradited eight Workers' Party rebels. This, Ocalan said, was the reason for the retaliation. Not long after the murder, police had taken thirteen Swedish Kurds into custody, but they had all been released without charge. The Kurds weren't the only ones who had a problem with Palme. He was a firm supporter of the anti-apartheid movement in South Africa. Only a week before his death he had hosted a major anti-

Left: A memorial stone in Stockholm marks the spot where Palme fell: "In this place, Sweden's prime minister, Olof Palme, was murdered."

apartheid conference in Stockholm where he spoke out against South Africa's racist system. There are many who believe he died at the hands of the South African Secret Police, who wanted to put an end to the secret financial contributions Palme was making to the anti-apartheid African National Congress. After the end of apartheid in 1994, veterans of the intelligence community in South Africa claimed their government was responsible, but investigations led nowhere and no hard evidence emerged.

The case may have gone cold, but the Swedes haven't given up hope. In November 2016 Swedish authorities announced that the investigation would be relaunched in February 2017 with successful prosecutor Krister Petersson running the show. With three decades' worth of files, taking up 820 feet of shelf space, to get through, the task is a daunting one, but it means this case might not stay unsolved for too much longer.

— STRANGE —
SUSPICION

Above: President of the Socialist Federal Republic of Yugoslavia, Josip Broz Tito (right), also known as Marshal Tito, pictured with the Vice President.

Lisbet Palme has said that she believes her husband was killed by right-wing Croatian separatists, and there is some evidence to support this theory. Until his death in 1980, the Socialist Federal Republic of Yugoslavia, made up of six socialist republics, including Croatia, was under the thumb of Marshal Tito and his secret police, the UDBA. Even after he died, a secret war continued to be waged around the world, as extremists attempted to stamp out Yugoslavian dissidents who had emigrated to the West. A number of these "enemies" of

the republic could be found in Sweden. Known attacks on Yugoslavians in Sweden include the 1972 assault on the embassy in Stockholm, during which the ambassador was assassinated. Croatian terrorists then hijacked a Scandinavian Airlines flight to force Sweden to release the perpetrators of the embassy attack. Under Palme's leadership, Sweden kept close tabs on Croatian extremists, with the help of the UDBA. Could his resolve to clamp down on terrorism have been the reason for his own assassination?

There's no hard evidence to back up the theory. But in 2011 a UDBA operative named Vinko Sindicic, who was serving fifteen years in prison in the U.K., claimed that it was Yugoslav secret service agents who killed Palme. Sindicic told a German news outlet they planned to pin the murder on right-wing Croatian separatists to help discredit their enemies. In the interview he named the assassin as "Ivo D" and claimed that he was now living in Croatia as a pensioner.

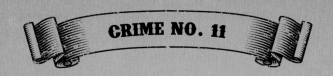

WHO KILLED HUNDREDS OF WOMEN IN THE MEXICAN CITY OF CIUDAD JUÁREZ?

Date: 1993 to present
Location: Ciudad Juárez, Mexico

When, in the 1990s, Ciudad Juárez's women started being murdered in their droves, the Mexican city faced a media storm and the start of a never-ending investigation.

In 1993, seventeen women were murdered in the north Mexico border city of Ciudad Juárez, Chihuahua. They had been shot, strangled, beaten, and even set on fire. In 1994, thirteen women suffered the same fate. And in 1995, a further twenty-three had been added to the list. While some were convinced this was the work of a serial killer, including state criminologist Oscar Maynez Grijalva, others have argued that the slayings, often referred to as feminicides, are the deeds of multiple killers, their crimes the result of deep-rooted societal attitudes.

Of the roughly three hundred women who were murdered in the city between 1993 and 2002, many were the victims of domestic violence, killed by a partner or ex-partner, but seventy-six of them were not. They were very young, dark-skinned, lanky women,

and had been raped before being strangled to death. Most of them were migrants, working in the foreign-owned assembly factories, known as *maquiladoras*, far from home with few friends or family to notice their disappearance. Because of the *maquiladoras'* locations, these women often had to walk home alone at night. Most of their bodies were found in the city's sprawling desert surroundings, and many weren't discovered until long after the elements had rendered them unrecognizable.

Above: In Ciudad Juárez, pink crosses mark the spots where women's bodies have been found and act as a symbol of anti-feminicide sentiment.

ABDUL LATIF SHARIF

Media coverage and international outrage put pressure on the authorities to find the killer. In 1995 the police got their first big lead. An Egyptian man, Abdul Latif Sharif, who had moved to the city in 1994, by way of the United States (where he had previous rape convictions and was in the process of being deported), was accused by a female resident of raping her and holding her captive in her own home. The investigating officers soon discovered that Sharif had been seen spending time with Elizabeth Castro García, a seventeen-year-old whose body had been discovered in August that year. Sharif received a thirty-year sentence for García's murder, the country's maximum penalty, and was named as a suspect in seventeen others.

The Mexican police must have thought they had their man, but the killings didn't stop when Sharif was behind bars. In the first nine months of his sentence, fifteen more women were killed. The police claimed that these new murders were being carried out by a street gang, *Los Rebeldes*, under Sharif's instruction from prison. They even went so far as to charge several members of the gang with conspiracy to free Sharif—a charge that was strongly denied and never went to trial.

MURDER BY NUMBERS

As the nineties drew to a close, the number of unsolved female murders was consistently high: in 1997 there were twenty; in 1998, twenty-one. And the murders continued into the 2000s. Even more women have simply disappeared, their bodies never discovered. The murders have been attributed to everything from gangland prostitution rings and traffickers to satanic cults and organ thieves. One theory is that the women's deaths are a form of blood sport for the city's elite.

Either way, the country's police forces are otherwise engaged, fighting the drug cartels and enforcing the border. It's important to remember that in Mexico very few crimes are successfully prosecuted. But *machista*—the word used to describe a cultural machismo that means Mexican men feel entitled to beat, rape, and kill women—seems ingrained in the way of life in Ciudad Juárez: the city has the highest levels of domestic violence in the country. Women are routinely blamed for their male relatives' struggles, while their own murders are blamed on their short skirts, choice of boyfriends, or the fact they were walking alone.

—STRANGE—
SUSPICION

Bus drivers have been implicated in the deaths of Ciudad Juárez's women more than once. In 1999, convicted rapist Jesús Manuel Guardado, who worked as a bus driver, fled after he became the prime suspect in the rape of a fourteen-year-old girl. When he was finally caught, he claimed four other bus drivers were responsible for the city's infamous killings. But none of these suspects have ever faced trial, and it's thought Guardado may have lied to lessen his own punishment. Was Guardado revealing the truth behind the murder spree or did he lie under duress to protect more powerful perpetrators?

In 2001, when the bodies of eight women were found on an overgrown parking lot in the heart of the city, it was as if someone was openly mocking the police. Only three days later, two bus drivers, Victor Javier García Uribe and Gustavo Gonzalez Meza, were arrested and allegedly confessed to the crime. Later they claimed they had been tortured into confessing, and shortly afterward

Above: The murders are mounting up in Mexico, with boxes of unsolved cases like these becoming depressingly common.

one of their defense team was killed in a high-speed car chase with the police. The families of the victims did not believe they were the killers. Gonzalez Meza died in police custody in 2003, and in 2004 García Uribe was sentenced to fifty years for the murders.

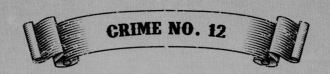

WHO KILLED JONBENÉT RAMSEY?

Date: December 26, 1996
Location: Boulder, Colorado, USA

In 1996, 804 children were murdered in the United States. But there's one child that the general public remembers to this day. Her name was JonBenét Ramsey.

At 5:52 a.m. on December 26, 1996, the Boulder, Colorado Police Department received an emergency call:

Patsy Ramsey: *"Police."*
911 dispatcher: *"What's going on there, Ma'am?"*
Patsy Ramsey: *"We have a kidnapping. Hurry, please!"*
911 dispatcher: *"Explain to me what's going on, OK?"*
Patsy Ramsey: *"There's a note left and our daughter's gone."*

Patsy and John Ramsey lived in a large house in a wealthy neighborhood of the city. They had two children together, a son, Burke, who was nine, and a daughter, JonBenét, who was six. Police arrived on the scene shortly after the 911 call. By then, two couples—the Whites and the Fernies—both friends of the Ramseys, had also arrived to show their support, contaminating the crime scene in the process. The police learned that Patsy had risen early—the family were due to leave for a trip to their summer home in Michigan—to find her daughter missing from her bed and a nearly three-page ransom note at the foot of the stairs. The long letter signed by "S. B. T. C.," which some think stands for "Saved by the cross," claimed to have been written by a "group of individuals that represent a small foreign faction." The author wrote that they had kidnapped JonBenét and that if the Ramseys wanted her returned unharmed, they should withdraw $118,000 from their bank account and wait for a phone call between 8 a.m. and 10 a.m. The letter warned the parents not to contact the authorities, saying their daughter would be killed if they did. Patsy called the police.

The 10 a.m. deadline passed without a phone call. Just before 1 p.m. Detective Linda Arndt told John Ramsey and his friend Fleet White to search the house again for any personal items that might have been stolen (as a way to keep John occupied). At 1:05 p.m. John found his daughter in an unfinished wine cellar in the house's large basement. He carried her body upstairs, placing it beneath the Christmas tree. What was potentially the scene of the murder had been irreparably contaminated.

JonBenét's body had been wrapped in a blanket. Her arms were tied above her head with cord, and a similar piece of cord was wrapped around her neck, with a garrote made from the handle of one of Patsy's paintbrushes. The autopsy revealed she had died by ligature strangulation, but she also had a fracture on the right side of her skull and other more minor abrasions on her skin.

Below: JonBenét Ramsey's death turned the attention of the world's media on the small city of Boulder, Colorado.

Unidentified DNA material (which was not blood, semen, or skin) was found beneath her fingernails and on her underwear.

THE PARENTS

Ninety-two percent of children found murdered in the family home are killed by a family member. So it was no surprise when the police's attention turned to the Ramseys. There were a number of factors that roused suspicion. When police arrived at the scene of the crime, Patsy had done her hair and makeup. Patsy's description of how she discovered the ransom note, in relation to when she had checked on her daughter, was inconsistent. John Ramsey had failed to report a broken basement window, which he had gone down and closed at 10 a.m. The ransom note itself—unusually long and rehearsed in nature—was written on paper from the Ramsey home using a pen found in their kitchen. And the unusual amount of money the kidnapper demanded was the same figure John Ramsey had received as his corporate bonus.

As the media circus descended on Boulder, stories about JonBenét and Patsy's volatile relationship started to surface. The former

Left: Patsy Ramsey died from ovarian cancer ten years after her daughter's murder.

Above: JonBenét Ramsey was murdered at her family home in Boulder, Colorado.

Miss West Virginia must have been jealous of her beauty pageant-winning daughter or frustrated with her bedwetting and had lashed out in a moment of rage, said the tabloids. The "kidnapping" was a cover-up, staged by the Ramseys. Police took handwriting samples from both parents. John's handwriting was quickly cleared by experts, but analysis of five samples of Patsy's writing provided an inconclusive result.

By the evening of December 26, the Ramseys had hired a lawyer. They refused to sit down for taped interviews with the police until four months after the murder. Their behavior in front of the cameras and in media interviews didn't live up to what the public expected from grieving parents, and they were quickly vilified. While they were never officially named as suspects, just "under the umbrella of suspicion," in the three years after the case, a hundred other people were cleared as suspects in the investigation; the Ramseys had to wait until 2008, twelve years after their daughter's death, to be officially absolved of any involvement in the crime.

Above: The Ramseys
declared their innocence
during a television
interview with local news
stations on May 2, 1997.

By then, Patsy Ramsey had passed away following a thirteen-year battle with ovarian cancer.

PROTECTING THEIR SON

JonBenét's parents weren't the only Ramseys to face media speculation. The child's older brother, Burke, was also thought to be a suspect. Theorists posited that Burke had been responsible for the blow to the head JonBenét received, using either a baseball bat found outside the house or a heavy flashlight that was on the kitchen counter—but no trace of JonBenét or Burke was discovered on either item. There were also reports that he had hit his sister with a golf club a week before her murder. Burke was also absolved by the District Attorney's office in 2008. In a 2016 CBS TV special investigation into the case, forensic experts pointed to the piece of undigested pineapple in JonBenét's intestines. They suggested that Burke had struck his sister after she snuck some of his late-night snack. Burke, then twenty-nine, filed a $750 million lawsuit against CBS and gave an exclusive interview to Dr. Phil in which he maintained his innocence.

With no one charged with the murder, in 1998 a grand jury was convened to examine the evidence. A grand jury can use its powers to subpoena information the police are unable to access, and can indict someone if it finds probable cause they committed the crime. The group of four men and eight women reviewed over 30,000 pages of reports and hundreds of pieces of evidence relating to the investigation. After thirteen months they found there was not enough evidence to charge anyone with the killing of JonBenét.

—STRANGE—
SUSPICION

The Ramseys, desperate to find their daughter's killer and focus the investigation away from themselves, accused their own friend, Fleet White; their housekeeper; and an elderly man who had dressed up as Santa at the party the family had attended on Christmas Day. A more likely suspect was Michael Helgoth, a local electrician who was involved in a property dispute with the Ramseys. Within two months of JonBenét's murder, Helgoth was dead in an apparent suicide. A stun gun was found in his apartment, as was a baseball cap with the letters SBTC on it and some Hi-Tec boots thought to match a print found in the Ramseys' basement. But Helgoth's DNA—and his death—cleared him as a suspect.

In August 2006 John Mark Karr, an American former teacher living in Bangkok, Thailand, was extradited and arrested as a suspect after claiming he had been with JonBenét when she died. He said he had killed her by accident, and that he loved her. However, after

Above: John Mark Karr, who claimed he was with JonBenét when she died, was never charged with her murder.

the former California teacher, who had been convicted of possessing child pornography in 2001, provided DNA samples for testing, investigators realized his story didn't add up, and he was subsequently released. It's thought Karr was obsessed with the case and had even sent letters to the Ramsey family before his arrest.

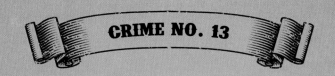
WERE THE MURDERS OF TUPAC SHAKUR AND BIGGIE SMALLS CONNECTED?

Date: September 7, 1996, and March 9, 1997
Location: Las Vegas, Nevada, and Los Angeles, California, USA

A hip-hop war that had been brewing for some time exploded on the Las Vegas Strip one night in 1996, and the repercussions were felt for years after.

On September 7, 1996, Mike Tyson was trying to win back the heavyweight championship he had lost six years earlier. The Las Vegas Strip was packed with celebrities in town to see him fight Bruce Seldon at the MGM Grand. Seated in one of the $1,000 ringside seats was actor and rapper Tupac Shakur. The fight was a disappointment—Tyson defeated Seldon in a speedy 109 seconds—but real violence, not sportsmanship, was what the evening would be remembered for.

In the MGM lobby, leaving the hotel, Shakur, who was a member of the LA street gang the Bloods, got into an altercation with Orlando Anderson, a member of rival gang the Crips. Shakur was with Death Row Records CEO Suge Knight, a bodyguard, and their crew, who proceeded to beat Anderson up, before Shakur made his way back to his hotel, the Luxor, to change. Knight met Shakur in the Luxor lobby around 11 p.m. They were heading to a benefit party at Knight's Club 662, and they got into a black BMW 750 and made their way down the Strip. Knight was driving and Shakur sat in the passenger seat with the windows rolled down.

DRIVE-BY SHOOTING

At 11:05 p.m. a bicycle cop stopped them for violating city noise laws but let them go without a ticket. About fifteen minutes later, they turned on to Flamingo Road, followed by an entourage of staff and groupies, and stopped at a red light. A white Cadillac with three or four men in it came to a stop beside them. Suddenly, the boxed-in BMW was sprayed with thirteen rounds from a high-powered semi-automatic handgun

brandished by a man in the back seat of the Cadillac. Both Knight and Shakur were hit. The latter took four shots—to the chest, pelvis, right hand, and thigh. The Cadillac, which was never found, sped off into the night, while Shakur was rushed to hospital. He remained there, largely in an unconscious state, for six days, and died from his injuries on September 13, 1996, aged twenty-five. Despite there being plenty of witnesses to the shooting, most of those who were present, including Knight, refused to talk to the police.

Above: Tupac Shakur was just twenty-five when he died from gunshot wounds.

Six months later, on March 9, 1997, Brooklyn-born hip-hop artist Christopher Wallace, who went by the names Biggie Smalls and The Notorious B. I. G., had been attending the Soul Train Awards in Los Angeles, California. Wallace left the event with his entourage traveling in two Chevy Suburbans. He was sitting in the front passenger seat of one car alongside associates of

Left: The Las Vegas intersection of Flamingo Road and Koval Lane where Knight and Shakur were shot.

his, and Sean "Puffy" Combs, who had signed Wallace to his Bad Boy Records label, was traveling with three bodyguards in the other vehicle. The cars were stopped at a red light outside the Petersen Automotive Museum on Wilshire Boulevard when, in a scene reminiscent of Shakur's killing, a Chevy Impala drove past and a man wearing a suit and bowtie opened fire. Wallace was struck by four GECO bullets, which easily pierced the car's metalwork. Three of these shots weren't fatal, but one to his abdomen perforated his colon, liver, heart, and left lung. He was pronounced dead at 1:15 a.m., aged twenty-four. The FBI thought the rare ammunition used, made only in Europe and sold in a few Californian and New Jersey stores, would help them find the killer, but no other crimes were committed using the same ammo and the lead led them nowhere.

No one has ever been arrested for the killing of either man—the stalled investigations were blamed on police prejudice and failure to secure evidence. But the loss of two of hip-hop's greatest talents has remained a conspiracy theorist's dream, with endless speculation as to who was behind the eerily similar murders.

Right: One of many Biggie Smalls murals celebrating the East Coast rapper.

A RAP RIVALRY

Shakur's death was not the start of an East Coast–West Coast rivalry, but it certainly fueled the flames ignited in 1994 when he had miraculously survived another shooting spree. The attack occurred during a visit to Manhattan's Quad Recording Studios to lay down a rap. His friend "Biggie" was there too, as was Combs.

Once Shakur arrived at the studio, a robbery ensued, carried out by two unknown men. Shakur resisted and was shot in the head, hand, and testicle—none of the bullets causing serious damage. Although the cops said it was a robbery gone awry, Shakur couldn't escape the feeling he'd been set up by Wallace and Combs. The song "Who Shot Ya?," put out by Wallace not long after the shooting, was thought to be a thinly veiled mockery of Shakur. The rivalry continued when Shakur released "Hit 'Em Up" in 1996, which alluded to him having an affair with Wallace's wife, Faith Evans.

At the time of Shakur's death in 1996, the 1994 shooting was still fresh in people's minds, and many people thought that his murder was a second orchestrated attempt on his life: this time,

Above: A former LAPD cop recently claimed that Sean Combs, who has gone by the stage names Puff Daddy, Puffy, and P. Diddy, was involved in Tupac's murder.

whoever wanted him dead was determined to see the job done. Sean Combs, who has also gone by the names P. Diddy and Puff Daddy, may have outlived his contemporaries, but he hasn't exactly gotten off lightly. As recently as 2016, a former LAPD cop, Greg Kading, who was on a special task force to investigate the murders, has claimed that Combs paid Crips gang member Duane Keith "Keffe D" Davis $1 million to carry out the murder. The theory goes that Knight's West Coast Death Row Records was too much competition for Combs's Bad Boy Records, and Davis reportedly overheard Combs saying he'd "give anything for Pac and Suge Knight's heads." The police officer claims that Davis's nephew, Orlando Anderson—who had been beaten up earlier in the evening—ended up being the shooter. Anderson strongly denied any involvement, claiming to be a fan of Shakur. He was killed in an unrelated 1998 gang shooting.

Despite the fact Shakur and Wallace were both so young when they died, they lived as if death could be just around the corner. Shakur had taken to wearing a Kevlar vest out of fear of being shot (although he wasn't wearing one that night in Vegas). After Wallace's death, Faith Evans talked about how he had also lived in fear after Tupac's murder. "I think it would be some element of fear that would kind of run through his mind," she said. "He was already getting threatening phone calls. I'm sure he thought he could be next." In 2015, reflecting back on what had happened, she said, "The only way you can look at it is tragic. Tragic and senseless. But I don't think that situation was the result of being in the music business. It's a little deeper than that."

— STRANGE —
SUSPICION

Two months after Tupac Shakur's death, his fifth album was released (the release date was brought forward by Knight). It sold 664,000 copies in its first week and became one of the top-selling hip-hop albums of all time. This surge in notoriety, resulting in huge profits for Death Row Records, has been used to support the idea that Suge Knight may have been behind Shakur's death, despite the fact he was also shot by the assailant. Reportedly, despite publicly declaring his loyalty to Knight and Death Row, Shakur, who'd been contractually bound to the label, was starting to consider other offers. If Knight didn't want his friend to migrate elsewhere, having him killed (and risking his own life in the process) was a pretty extreme step to take.

Whether he was behind Shakur's death or not, Knight has also had the finger pointed at him for Wallace's death. It's been alleged that Knight hired Bloods gang member Wardell "Poochie" Fouse to take out Wallace in retaliation for

Above: Co-founder and CEO of Death Row Records, Suge Knight, has had the finger pointed at him for both murders.

Shakur's death. He reportedly paid him $13,000 for the murder. Fouse died in a shooting in 2003 from multiple gunshot wounds. Knight has been facing life in prison since January 2015, when he was charged with murder and attempted murder after an unrelated hit-and-run in Los Angeles.

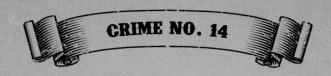

WHO ORDERED THE MURDER OF ANNA POLITKOVSKAYA?

Date: October 7, 2006
Location: Moscow, Russia

Journalist Anna Politkovskaya did her job: she reported the truth that some people didn't want the world to hear. For this, she paid with her life.

A nna Politkovskaya was a highly respected journalist among many of her Russian colleagues and around the world, but not everyone approved of her work. "In Moscow, I am not invited to press conferences or gatherings that Kremlin officials might attend," she wrote in an essay two months before she died, "in case the organizers are suspected of harboring sympathies toward me." Politkovskaya worked for the independent *Novaya Gazeta* and was a staunch critic of President Vladimir Putin. She was known for her fearless reporting of Russia's involvement in the Chechen war. In short, there were many powerful people who opposed her work and her point of view.

On October 7, 2006, Politkovskaya was planning a trip to the hospital to visit her mother, who had recently been diagnosed with cancer. Two weeks earlier, Anna's father had died of a heart attack. She had something to look forward to, however: her twenty-six-year-old daughter was pregnant and staying with her. The journalist had a deadline the next day for her latest story, so instead of going to the hospital she went to a grocery store to pick up supplies and headed home. She lived on the seventh floor, so picked up half her shopping and went up in the elevator, leaving the groceries outside her apartment before getting back into the elevator to head down and collect the rest.

When the doors opened on the ground floor, Politkovskaya came face to face with her killer. She was shot four times with a silencer-equipped IZH pistol. The first three bullets went through her heart, lungs, and shoulder, throwing her toward the back of the elevator. The assassin then delivered the *kontrolnyi vystrel*—the control shot—a bullet to the head from just a few inches away. He dropped the weapon and left the scene. The death had all the hallmarks of a professional killing. Someone had been paid to silence Politkovskaya forever.

Above: Russian journalist Anna Politkovskaya worked for the independent *Novaya Gazeta* newspaper when she was murdered.

A DANGEROUS LIFE

Before her murder, Politkovskaya had learned to live with the continuous threat of violence and death. She regularly received obscene phone calls in the night and anonymous emails describing her fate, and after being arrested by the military while reporting in Chechnya, she experienced a mock execution. In 2001, after she'd accused a special services police officer of committing atrocities against civilians, she received email threats claiming he would exact his revenge. She fled to Austria, probably hoping the threats would come to nothing. Then a woman who looked similar to her was

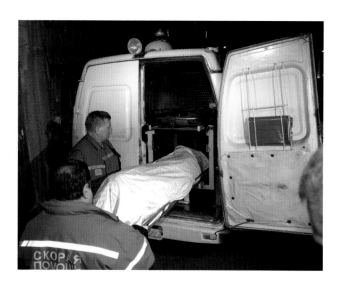

Above: Politkovskaya's body being taken away by paramedics after she was murdered at her apartment building.

killed in front of her apartment building in Moscow. In 2004 she was on her way to Beslan in North Ossetia, where an Islamic group had taken 1,100 people hostage in a school. It's thought the Russian army, which has come under criticism for its handling of the crisis, didn't want journalists there. On the flight Politkovskaya saw three men she described as members of the FSB, the Russian security service. Ten minutes after drinking some tea she started to lose consciousness. When she awoke in the hospital, the nurse whispered to her, "My dear, they tried to poison you." The doctors told her all of her blood tests and medical records from her time there were destroyed on orders "from on high."

POLITICAL REACTION

When Politkovskaya was shot, memorial services were held in Paris and New York, among other places, but President Putin acted as if nothing had happened. Four days after the fact, while on state business in Germany, he attended a press conference and was asked directly about the killing. While he acknowledged that "this is a horribly cruel crime," he was just as quick to call Politkovskaya "too radical."

It's possible the FSB finally decided that enough was enough—Politkovskaya's writing abroad was garnering too much attention and she was becoming too much of a liability to the Kremlin. Or perhaps her reporting on Chechnya had angered pro-Russian Chechen leaders? Both Prime Minister Ramzan Kadyrov and President Alu Alkhanov (both pro-Moscow) were quick to condemn her murder, but just as quick to absolve themselves of any guilt. Kadyrov said that presumptions about Chechnya's involvement were "not based on serious evidence … and unworthy of the press and politicians." In the last article Politkovskaya wrote she condemned the widespread human rights abuses committed in the North Caucasus region by Chechen forces loyal to Mr. Kadyrov.

The Russian investigation into Politkovskaya's murder focused immediately on her investigative reporting as a motive for the crime. One of her newspaper's shareholders offered a $1 million reward to anyone who could solve it. There was CCTV footage showing a woman and a man wearing a baseball cap following Politkovskaya in the grocery store, and of the same man entering her building after her. But despite this, and the fact that Prosecutor-General Yury Chaika (the most powerful person in the Russian justice system) took charge of the investigation, it would be eight years before any justice was done.

In 2014 Moscow's highest criminal court sentenced five men to prison for their involvement in Politkovskaya's death. Rustam Makhmudov was found guilty of the shooting itself, while the other four were convicted for organizing the killing. The court ruled that they were part of a conspiracy to assassinate her, and two of them received life-term prison sentences. These men, however, were not the masterminds behind the murder. They were merely fulfilling a contract on someone else's orders. Until the person who ordered the hit is brought to justice, the case remains unsolved.

Below: On the seventh anniversary of Politkovskaya's death, a memorial plaque was unveiled outside the *Novaya Gazeta* offices in Moscow.

RISKY BUSINESS

Politkovskaya was not the first journalist killed for doing her job, and she won't be the last. According to the Committee to Protect Journalists, since 1992, fifty-six journalists have been killed in Russia, and thirty-six of these have been murdered. In 2010 the Russian government made a public commitment to pursue nineteen cases of murdered journalists, but the country still remains one of the most dangerous places in the world in terms of freedom of expression for the press.

"Anna knew the risks only too well," her sister, Elena Kudimova, told the *New Yorker* magazine in an interview published a few months after Politkovskaya's death. She explained how Anna had even obtained a U.S. passport after her family had insisted upon it. "We all begged her to stop," said Kudimova. "But she always answered the same way: 'How could I live with myself if I didn't write the truth?'"

Below: The four men found guilty of organizing the killing of Politkovskaya. The convicted shooter is not pictured.

— STRANGE — SUSPICION

Above: Politkovskaya pictured at the memorial plaque for the victims of the Dubrovka Theater siege.

Politkovskaya wrote openly and honestly about life in Russia, but some think one particular Pandora's box that she opened could have been the cause of her death. In October 2002, Chechen rebels laid siege to a Moscow theater for 57 hours. Of the 850–900 hostages, at least 130 died, along with the terrorists, after the Russian military pumped toxic gas into the theater to flush out the rebels. It was a difficult time for Putin's presidency, but the hasty government investigation found no wrongdoing, and the Russian authorities presented their handling of the event as a victory. However, an independent investigation, which Politkovskaya was involved with, proved that on some level the Russian secret services had collaborated with the terrorists.

In 2003, Politkovskaya met with Khanpash Terkibayev, a Chechen man who said he had been part of the terrorist team behind the siege. The account he gave to Politkovskaya, which he later denied, revealed the FSB were involved with the planning of the siege and that it was largely staged. His honesty may have cost him his life: he was killed in a car crash in 2004. Others involved in the unofficial investigation—politician Sergei Yushenkov and former FSB agent Alexander Litvinenko—were both murdered. The former was shot dead in Moscow and the latter died in London of polonium poisoning a few weeks after Politkovskaya was killed. Perhaps these deaths were all linked by their insistence in seeking the truth about what had happened that week at the theater.

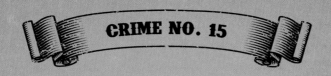
WHAT IS THE EXPLANATION FOR THE SALISH SEA FEET MYSTERY?

Date: August 20, 2007, to present
Location: Salish Sea, North America

When human feet started washing ashore on Canada's west coast, many thought a serial killer was responsible. How else to explain where all these feet were coming from?

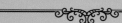

On a summer's day in 2007, a father took his daughter on a Salish Sea boat trip from Washington State up to Canada's Georgia Strait. They were cruising past Jedediah Island when they came across a shoe floating in the water. Curious, the girl took a look inside and found a sock. When she looked further she made a shocking discovery: what remained of the owner's foot was still inside.

It was a right foot, size 12, preserved inside a blue and white Campus running shoe, made and distributed largely in India in 2003. The mystery was compounded a few weeks later when a second size-12 foot was discovered on nearby Gabriola Island, also inside a running shoe. It was also a right foot, but the foot did not belong to the same individual. And the feet kept coming. By the

Right: The Salish Sea feet all had one thing in common: they were all wearing sneakers or running shoes.

end of 2008, four more had been discovered in the region and one across the border on the U.S. shore. Of those seven feet, there were two pairs, one of which belonged to a woman. The rest of the feet had come from men.

Between 2007 and 2016 at least thirteen human feet have been found in the region. When the first few were discovered, authorities thought they might be facing a serial killer with a foot fetish or a running joke being carried out by medical students. However, it soon became apparent that the feet had not been cut off in a violent attack or amputated by professionals; they had naturally separated from the rest of the body after being at sea. Forensics experts are able to tell by looking at the end of a bone whether it has disarticulated naturally or whether a force or injury has been applied to it.

SHOE CLUE

Other than the general area they were found in, the one thing the feet all had in common was the type of footwear they had on: sneakers and running shoes. Many of the shoes were no longer in production or were only available in certain countries, which helped the police to narrow down the potential origin of the owner,

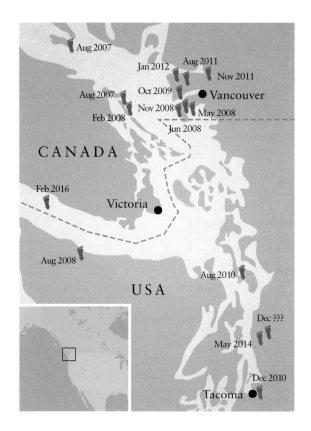

Above: This map shows the discovery spots of the thirteen feet found between August 2007 and February 2016.

as well as the date they may have died. The athletic footwear, which many thought was the link to a killer's identity—someone picking off runners out in the wild—was actually the reason these feet were found in the first place.

Every year thousands of people die at sea. Almost immediately, those bodies are broken down by the oceans' scavengers over a period as short as a few days to as much as a few months. But a foot encased in a sock and a shoe is better protected from the water and the sea life that sees it as dinner. The tissue just wasn't being eaten. In some cases the feet had saponified, a chemical reaction that transforms the fatty tissue into soap. Once this has happened, the tissue is not enticing to any scavengers. Experts believe the uptick of foot discoveries from 2007 is to do with the materials and construction of athletic footwear in more recent years. Sports shoes are now made using hi-tech foam with lots of air pockets, and the lightness that makes them great for athletes also turns them into flotation devices when they're in the water. British Columbia (BC) is not the only part of the world where solitary feet are washed up, but the high number of incidents there has been attributed to the tide and current patterns, and to the fact that media attention surrounding the stories makes beach walkers more vigilant in spotting them.

As feet have continued to surface over the years, conspiracy theorists have pointed to natural disasters, drug gangs, aliens,

— STRANGE —
SUSPICION

Above: Clover Point beach in Victoria, BC, where children's shoes were found stuffed with animal flesh and bones in an unsavory prank.

In 2012 five child-sized shoes were found in the Clover Point beach area, BC. The shoes were stuffed with flesh and bones, terrifying the community. Perhaps the Salish Sea killer was bored of trail runners and had turned their attention to children. Luckily, police soon ascertained that the flesh was not human. For some unsavory types, the Salish Sea feet had provided the perfect setup for a troublesome hoax. But the prank was not taken lightly. "I don't care what it takes," said a police constable investigating the case, "we need to find these people and need to bring them to justice ... if you are going to be out there doing this, we're going to come for you." And this wasn't the first foot-based hoax in the area. In June 2008 a sneaker was found washed up on the shores of BC's Campbell River with bones and seaweed inside. Further analysis revealed the bones weren't human—it was just a cruel trick.

and human traffickers as the cause, but using DNA profiling, police have been able to identify six people, some of whom had been missing or presumed dead for many years. Once these individuals were identified, it became much more apparent that these were not murder victims or alien abductees, but people who had died either by suicide or by accident, for example, in a coastal storm.

TERRORISM

When individuals commit unfathomable acts—destroying a city block or shooting a commercial airliner out of the sky—oftentimes their motivations go beyond the sadistic acts of violence perpetrated by murderers and serial killers. Their decision to bring destruction and devastation to the lives of innocent people they have never met is based on a matter of principle. Be it political, religious, or otherwise, terrorists strike fear into the hearts of the communities they ruin and the ones they have yet to, in large part because their crimes are so random. They are rogue acts of war, operating outside of the rules of warfare; they are violent protests with no concern for the hundreds of lives they leave shattered in their wake.

Left: The Cooperative Bank building in Nairobi, Kenya, towers over the remains of the damaged U.S. embassy after a terrorist bombing in 1998.

While terrorism can come in a number of forms, one of the factors that binds most terrorist acts is the fact that those responsible tend to lay claim to their "victories." Terrorist groups want the world to know that they were behind an attack. By taking credit for the damage, they seek to cement their reputation and further their cause. More rarely, no one wants to take the blame. The perpetrators prefer instead to let others take the fall, as in the case of the Birmingham Six, in the UK, or as could be seen after the East African U.S. embassy bombings, knowing that while some of the culprits might be caught, international borders and their own networks will protect the architects of these horrors.

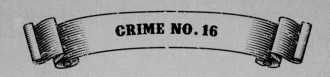

WHO WAS RESPONSIBLE FOR THE WALL STREET BOMBING?

Date: September 16, 1920
Location: New York City, USA

After years of anti-capitalist demonstrations, Wall Street felt the full wrath of anarchic terror delivered by the most innocent of means: a horse and cart.

The September 11 attack on the World Trade Center in 2001 is the terrorist atrocity New York City will forever be associated with, but eighty-one years before the Twin Towers were hit, the Big Apple was the scene of a possible terror attack that has long been forgotten in the annals of history. September 16, 1920, started like any other busy New York day. The lunch rush was just getting going in the financial district when a nondescript man driving a horse and red cart, with a heavy load, parked up on the corner of Broad and Wall, outside the U.S. Assay Office—where bullion deposits were received from mining prospectors—and the J. P. Morgan building at number 23 Wall Street. He got out quickly and disappeared into the crowd, leaving his horse and cart behind. Inside the cart was a bomb made from an estimated hundred sticks of dynamite and 500 pounds of small

Right: Chaos on Wall Street in the aftermath of the blast in 1920. Federal Hall can be seen in the background.

iron weights—shrapnel intended to cause serious harm. At 12:01 p.m. the timer on the bomb ticked down to zero.

"It was a crush out of a blue sky—an unexpected death-dealing bolt," said one witness, describing the explosion that followed. "Looking down Wall Street later I could see arising from the vicinity ... a mushroom-shaped cloud of yellowish, green smoke which mounted to a height of more than 100 feet, the smoke being licked by darting tongues of flame." The blast was unprecedented and the carnage unimaginable. Thirty people were killed instantly and hundreds more were injured by the shrapnel and destruction (the final death toll was thirty-eight). Office buildings blocks away had their windows shattered. The bomber's horse was decapitated; its hooves were found on different blocks in four directions. J. P. Morgan's chief clerk, Thomas Joyce, was among those who lost their lives that day, and Morgan's son, Junius, was injured.

After the attack, New Yorkers were keen to get back to business as usual and reopen the stock exchange. So city officials swept

Left: Police rope off the public and reporters from the debris and dead bodies in the aftermath of the explosion.

up the debris, effectively destroying most of the physical evidence that might have helped them to establish a suspect. A three-year investigation followed, but no one was ever charged and no suspects were ever officially identified. The Bureau of Investigation interviewed hundreds of witnesses, but few had recollections of the innocuous cart driver. The NYPD was able to reconstruct the bomb and its fuse mechanism, but all the components were commonly available and the investigation soon dried up.

AN ATTACK ON CAPITALISM

The J. P. Morgan building—and what it stood for—was the obvious target. Morgan, Jr., head of the bank, was in Europe at the time of the explosion, but had survived an attempt on his life a year earlier when Eric Muenter broke into Morgan's mansion in Glen Cove, Long Island, and shot him twice. Muenter was a German-American activist who was angered by the fact that Morgan and other bankers were profiting by lending money to the Allies during World War One. He thought by taking out the man at the top, he could potentially bring about the end of the war by crippling the Allies' finances. Anti-capitalist bombings and leftist riots were not new: they had been going on for nearly forty years at this point, including the Haymarket bombing in Chicago in 1886 and the bombing of the Los Angeles Times building in 1910. And these coordinated political attacks were becoming more common.

The Wall Street bombing caused in the region of $2 million worth of damage, but with the majority of victims being lowly workers and messenger boys, the attack didn't stem the tide of capitalism, as most people, bandaged and bruised, returned to work the next day. Thousands of people gathered at the site of the bombing to pay their respects, and a band played "The Star-Spangled Banner" while the crowds sang along. The stock market soared and as the Roaring Twenties ploughed ahead, so too did the economy.

As no one claimed responsibility, the public were left to make their own minds up about what had happened. Many thought that the perpetrators were communist agitators, transplants from the Bolshevik Revolution. In November 1919, after a summer that saw a mail-bomb plot and an attack on the home of Attorney General Mitchell Palmer, U.S. authorities raided the headquarters of the Union of Russian Workers in New York City and arrested and deported 249 radicals. There was a growing fear of foreign radicals, and a day after the Wall Street attack the *New York*

Right: A car overturned by the power of the explosion, which took the lives of thirty-eight people.

Above: On the wall at 23 Wall Street, the impact of the bombing can still be seen.

Times reported that "both the police and the government investigators were inclined to the theory that Reds had placed a time bomb in the wagon," further fueling speculation. But it was another European group that made the more likely suspects.

ITALIAN ANARCHISTS

One of the most promising leads in the case was a clue from before the bomb even went off. A letter carrier found four flyers in the area, distributed by a group called American Anarchist Fighters, demanding the release of political prisoners. The flyers were similar to some used the previous year in two bombing campaigns by Italian anarchists. The Bureau, now the FBI, was unable to locate where the flyers had been printed, but they were left in little doubt as to who was responsible: followers of the Italian anarchist Luigi Galleani, who had been deported to Italy in 1919. In 1944, the Bureau reopened the case and came to the conclusion that Italian anarchists were most likely behind the bombing. Unfortunately, there was no solid evidence to point the finger at any individuals.

Unlike atrocities in Western cities in more recent years, there is no plaque to mark the site of the explosion and no memorial to those who lost their lives. The Wall Street bombing remained the deadliest attack on American soil for 75 years, until the 1995 truck bombing at the Alfred P. Murrah Federal Building in Oklahoma City, which claimed the lives of 168 people. However, the signs of the 1920 attack are still there if you look hard enough. The pockmarked limestone facade at 23 Wall Street still bears the shrapnel scars from that fateful day.

STRANGE
SUSPICION

Despite the very deliberate positioning of the cart, and the bomb remnants, there were some who thought that perhaps the explosion had been an accident, and that J. P. Morgan wasn't targeted at all. The theory goes that during the post-War building boom, a cart full of explosives was not out of the ordinary, and this particular cart was part of a thriving underground trade. Department of Justice agent Frank Francisco was quoted in the *New York Times* saying, "If an attempt had been made on the Morgan offices, I believe it would have been made at night, or some radical would have secured a position in the institution and planted an infernal machine inside." The agent's intuition was probably based on the fact a lot of previous attacks had been much more heavily targeted to assassinate an individual or group of people. The victims of the Wall Street bomb were tourists, messengers, and World War One veterans who had survived the atrocities of the battlefield and were

Above: Was the explosion an accident? People couldn't believe an individual would deliberately maim so many innnocent bystanders.

now working in the Financial District. Many people found it hard to believe that a radicalized individual could deliberately hurt so many innocent people, as, unlike today, this level of mass violence was highly unusual. Even many years later, on the eve of the fortieth anniversary of the bombings, *Daily News* reporter Ruth Reynolds tracked down a member of the New York bomb squad who had been on the scene. When she asked him who he thought might have been the culprit, he replied that the explosion had been "an accident—pure and simple."

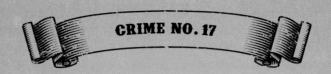

WHO WERE THE REAL BIRMINGHAM PUB BOMBERS?

Date: November 21, 1974
Location: Birmingham, UK

It was one of the deadliest terrorist attacks on British soil, but the Birmingham bombings are better known for the miscarriage of justice that followed.

It was 8:11 p.m. on a Thursday night in Birmingham city center when a man with an Irish accent called the *Evening Mail* and the *Birmingham Post* to tell them two bombs had been planted in the Rotunda building and in a tax office on New Street. He didn't provide the specific locations of the bombs, but he did sign off with the official code word "Double X," which was used by the Provisional Irish Republican Army (IRA) when they issued a warning call. This was no hoax.

The Provisional IRA wanted Northern Ireland to be part of an independent Ireland, rather than under British rule. Between 1968 and 1998 the group perpetrated a number of devastating bomb attacks, both in Northern Ireland and in mainland Britain. Traditionally the IRA would abide by its own code of conduct and

Right: The Tavern in the Town pub on New Street in the aftermath of the blast.

issue an adequate warning, usually thirty minutes before a device was set to detonate, to allow civilians to be evacuated. But on November 21, 1974, the warning came too late. Just six minutes after the newspapers received the call to tell them that an attack was imminent, a bomb exploded at the Mulberry Bush pub. Just ten minutes later a second bomb exploded at the nearby Tavern in the Town pub on New Street. The blast was so powerful it made a crater 3.5 feet deep in the floor. At 9:15 p.m. a third bomb, which had failed to go off, was found in the doorway of a bank two miles away. Twenty-one people were killed and 182 suffered serious injuries.

ADMITTING GUILT

Despite the bombing bearing many of the hallmarks of an IRA attack, the group denied responsibility. But that didn't stop police arresting five Northern Irish men at a ferry port later that evening. They were on their way to the funeral of an IRA member who had blown himself up while assembling a bomb. They'd taken a train from Birmingham New Street train station at 7:55 p.m., less than twenty minutes before the bombs had exploded. A sixth man was arrested the following evening.

All of the Birmingham Six, as they became known, were Republican sympathizers, living in the Midlands city since the 1960s, but none of them were members of the IRA. In custody they were threatened and tortured by police officers, which caused four of them to sign false confessions. The men, who maintained their innocence, were charged with twenty-one counts of murder and found guilty after a forty-five-day trial. After spending sixteen years in prison they were finally successful in appealing their case and in 1991 their convictions were overturned. New evidence had come to light which conclusively showed collusion and corruption among police officers involved with the case, finally proving that the men were not in any way involved.

Above: The Birmingham Six were Republican sympathizers but not members of the IRA.

The Birmingham Six were tried alongside three other men, including Mick Murray, who was charged with conspiracy to cause explosions. He was also found guilty but, unlike the "Six," he is now believed to have been the mastermind behind the attacks, and the person who made the phone call to the papers. It's thought he chose to catch a bus to his local pub before making the call, because the phone boxes nearer the bomb site were out of order. Unofficial investigations have named the perpetrators many now believe to be responsible, including Murray and Sean McLoughlin, both of whom are dead, and three other men who cannot be named for legal reasons. It's thought they are now living in the Republic of Ireland, but unless they hand themselves in and confess, there's little chance they'll ever be brought to justice. According to ex-IRA intelligence chief Kieran Conway, the men were just carrying out the instructions of their commanders. Their only fault, he said, was not checking that the phone boxes were working.

— STRANGE —
SUSPICION

In November 2016 it was announced that a new inquest into the deaths of those killed in the bombings would be opened. The senior coroner for the region, Louise Hunt, held a number of review hearings in the lead-up to the announcement, in which "significant" new information about the attacks came to light. Most pointedly, she said that questions needed answering about what warnings the police had been given that an attack was imminent. "I have serious concerns that advanced notice of the bombs may have been available to the police and that they failed to take the necessary steps to protect life," she said. It's possible the police knew all along that Birmingham pubs would be under attack, but why would they keep the news under wraps when the public were at risk? The inquest, which has not begun at the time of writing, will hopefully answer claims that the police knew what was going to happen because of a mole, but rather than blow the mole's cover they

Above: Paddy Hill, one of the Birmingham Six, campaigned alongside victims' families for a new inquest into the deaths.

framed the Birmingham Six instead. Unfortunately, some files relating to the case are under embargo for seventy-five years, and thirty-five pieces of important evidence have been lost, including the unexploded bomb. So even with the new inquest, it's possible we will never know if this was a scandalous cover-up or just bad police work.

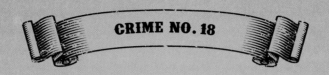

WHO WAS RESPONSIBLE FOR THE EAST AFRICAN U.S. EMBASSY BOMBINGS?

Date: August 7, 1998
Location: Dar es Salaam, Tanzania, and Nairobi, Kenya

The destruction caused by the simultaneous U.S. embassy bombings in East Africa shocked the world. Observers wondered who would dare to attack the world's biggest superpower.

A typical morning in Kenya's capital, Nairobi, turned into something resembling a war zone when, on August 7, 1998, at 10:35 a.m., a blast ripped through the city. Ten minutes later, nearly 435 miles away in neighboring Tanzania, in the busy capital of Dar es Salaam, another bomb went off. Both bombs were located next to United States embassies, leaving little room for doubt: this was a highly sophisticated, targeted terrorist operation.

In Nairobi, the 660-pound bomb had been planted in a Mitsubishi Pajero truck, parked in an alleyway between the embassy and Ufundi House, a five-story office block that was home to a number of small businesses and a secretarial college. The U.S. embassy was seriously damaged—its bulletproof doors ripped from their hinges—and two passing buses were also destroyed.

Over four thousand people were injured in the blast, but the majority of the 213 people who died in Nairobi were Kenyans working in Ufundi House. The building caved in, crushing many people to death. The blast was heard up to 10 miles away, and a thick cloud of smoke rose up over the city. Scores of locals were injured by flying glass as the explosion caused windows to blow out up to five blocks away. The U.S. ambassador, Prudence Bushnell, was meeting the Kenyan trade minister, Joseph Kamotho, at a nearby bank at the time and received minor injuries.

In Tanzania, support communications officer Vella G. Mbenna was working at the embassy and was on the telephone when the bomb went off. In a 2016 interview she described what happened next: "Before I finished the sentence, the blast occurred, because the wall I was facing came back in my face and slammed me into racks of equipment across the room." After Mbenna had assessed the communication center, she made her way toward the exit. "When I turned the corner, I saw the devastation that had occurred … It was like a meteorite had hit the embassy. Even worse was that the entire wall and windows facing the road was gone." The Tanzanian attack killed eleven people and injured eighty-five.

Above: Osama bin Laden was known to the international intelligence community, and it's believed he was behind the embassy bombings in East Africa.

THE WORK OF OSAMA BIN LADEN?

The United States was pretty sure who was to blame. Osama bin Laden had come to the intelligence community's attention after the 1993 bombing of the World Trade Center in New York. It was suspected that he was involved in international terrorism against the United States; since 1991 he had spoken out against the Saudi Arabian government and the U.S.'s continued military presence there, in his home country. His military organization, al-Qaeda, which he had set up during the Soviet occupation of Afghanistan,

Left: Clearing up after the attack— $4.3 million was spent by the U.S. to rebuild the center of Nairobi.

was still in existence, and was transforming into an anti-U.S. terrorist network. In 1995, bin Laden had incited guerilla attacks against U.S. troops in Saudi Arabia. It's also possible he was involved in planning a truck bombing that in 1996 killed nineteen military personnel stationed there. He had provided funding to the Islamic extremist group the Taliban, and had issued a religious decree six months prior to the embassy bombings calling for Muslims to kill Americans, including civilians, anywhere in the world. August 7, 1998, the day of the embassy bombings in East Africa, marked the eighth anniversary of the deployment of U.S. forces to Saudi Arabia.

Days after the devastation in East Africa, two of bin Laden's associates were arrested and charged with the attacks. And on August 20, President Bill Clinton ordered a retaliatory military strike in Afghanistan, where seventy American cruise missiles blew up what were thought to be al-Qaeda training camps, killing twenty-four people. But bin Laden was still at large. This didn't stop the U.S. from indicting him and twenty-one others in November that year, charging them with the two embassy bombings and conspiring to commit other acts of terrorism against

Americans abroad. It was February 2001 before four of these suspects—Mohamed Rashed Daoud al-'Owhali, Khalfan Khamis Mohamed, Wadih al-Hage, and Mohamed Sadeek Odeh—went on trial in New York. They were charged with 302 criminal counts related to the embassy attacks. While two of the men admitted they had ties to bin Laden, they claimed not to have been involved; the other two defendants admitted their involvement but said they had not engaged in a conspiracy against the U.S. On May 29 all four men were convicted on all charges and received sentences of life imprisonment. Exactly fifteen weeks later, on September 11, the United States would face the deadliest foreign attack on American soil since the bombing of Pearl Harbor. Nearly three thousand people were killed by the actions of nineteen al-Qaeda terrorists, and the embassy bombings, devastating as they were, paled in comparison.

WARNING SIGNS

There are some that think the atrocities in East Africa could have been prevented. As early as 1997, U.S. intelligence knew that bin Laden operatives were active in the region. And there had been warnings about the vulnerability of the Nairobi embassy in particular.

Right: The effects of the bombings were deeply felt by local communities, more so as it's believed the devastation could have been prevented.

Nine months prior to the attack, U.S. intelligence officials had received a warning that extremists were plotting to blow up the building from an Egyptian man named Mustafa Mahmoud Said Ahmed, who was later jailed for his involvement in the bombings. In the immediate aftermath, the U.S. State Department maintained that it had received no warnings about those embassies specifically, but in October 1998 it acknowledged that the CIA had sent two reports about Ahmed, causing security measures at the Kenyan embassy to be stepped up temporarily. When no attack occurred, the temporary security measures were abandoned and things returned to normal, with no permanent changes to the building's security. Ambassador Bushnell had even asked for the embassy to be relocated; unfortunately, her request was denied.

Osama bin Laden never claimed credit for the embassy bombings, but that wouldn't prevent him from being pursued relentlessly by the U.S. intelligence services. After ten years spent in hiding, following the September 11 attacks, for which he did claim responsibility, he was assassinated by U.S. forces at his compound in Abbottabad, Pakistan.

Left: Air strikes on al-Qaeda training bases in Sudan and Afghanistan took place two weeks after the bombings.

— STRANGE —
SUSPICION

President Bill Clinton was quick to condemn the embassy attacks, saying, "These acts of terrorist violence are abhorrent; they are inhuman ... We will use all the means at our disposal to bring those responsible to justice." Nine hundred FBI officials were sent to East Africa to investigate the attacks, but the $4.3 million spent by the U.S. to help rebuild central Nairobi was felt to be too little by some survivors, who tried unsuccessfully to sue the U.S. government. Given that a Tomahawk missile cost about $569,000 in 1999, and seventy were dropped on al-Qaeda training bases in Sudan and Afghanistan on August 20 (at an estimated cost of nearly $40 million), it's not hard to see why some felt cheated.

For many, the U.S. military campaign after the bombings was too hasty. Some joked that the war was "for Monica's eyes," mocking the affair scandal surrounding President Clinton at the time. Others thought the timing of the U.S. attacks was intended to distract

Above: Bill Clinton was a laughing stock after the revelations about his affair with Lewinsky. Was the military campaign an attempt to save face?

the international media from the affair. The day before the embassy bombings, the president's former intern, Monica Lewinsky, had testified to the grand jury about her relationship with the president. And on August 17, just three days before the retaliation on al-Qaeda, Clinton became the first sitting president to testify before a grand jury investigating his conduct. One Egyptian commentator went so far as to suggest the CIA carried out the embassy bombing to "divert what is happening in Washington."

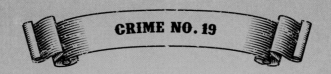

WHO SHOT DOWN MALAYSIA AIRLINES FLIGHT 17 OVER UKRAINE?

Date: July 17, 2014
Location: Airspace over Eastern Ukraine

When a commercial airliner fell from the sky in the Ukraine, people's first thoughts were of mechanical failure. The reality, however, was much more terrifying.

There were 283 passengers, including eighty children, and fifteen crew members on board the Boeing 777-200ER that left Schiphol Airport in Amsterdam at 12:31 p.m. local time. Malaysia Airlines Flight MH17 was due to arrive at Kuala Lumpur International airport 11 hours and 40 minutes later—but it never made it. Nearly three hours after takeoff, when the plane was 30 miles from the Russia–Ukraine border, it lost contact with air traffic control. Soon footage had emerged of a plane crash in the Donetsk area of Ukraine: the wreckage lay burning in a field in a region controlled by pro-Russian separatists. Bodies, which had been thrown from the plane, were strewn around it.

A fifteen-month investigation followed. It was undertaken by the Netherlands' Dutch Safety Board (DSB), at the request of the

Ukraine government, because most of the passengers were Dutch citizens. In October 2015 the DSB released its findings. They showed the plane had followed a typical flight path to Asia and was cruising at an altitude of 33,000 feet when it entered Ukrainian airspace. The crew had to divert from the path slightly to avoid some thunderstorms, but returned to it shortly after. Because there was a conflict between the Ukrainian government and pro-Russian separatist groups in the region, the airspace at 32,000 feet and below was restricted for commercial traffic, but MH17 was routed above this height when it was shot down.

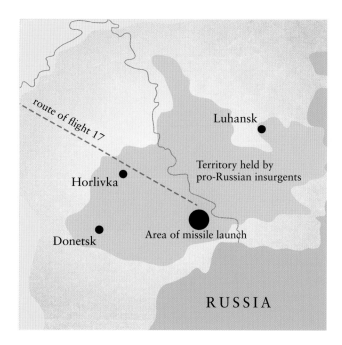

Above: This map shows the flight path MH17 was on when it was shot down over pro-Russian separatist territory.

After the wreckage was recovered, investigators were able to determine the type of weapon used: a Russian-made 9N314M-type warhead, which was carried on a 9M38M1 missile. The warhead had been launched from an SA-11 Buk anti-aircraft missile system, of the type used by both Russia and Ukraine. Using simulation software, investigators were able to establish that the warhead had exploded about 13 feet above the airplane's nose, to the left of the cockpit. The front of the plane was hit by hundreds of "high-energy objects" from the warhead, killing the crew and causing the cockpit and then the tail section to break away. Between a minute and 90 seconds later, the rest of the plane crashed upside down.

WHO FIRED THE MISSILE?

Based on the location of the plane when it lost contact with air traffic control and where the wreckage was found, the location

Above: Pro-Russian sentiment escalated into protests and military action in Ukraine in 2014. Here the protestors are replacing a Ukrainian flag with a Russian one.

of the missile launcher was narrowed down to an area of east Ukraine that measures 124 square miles. The Joint Investigation Team (JIT), which consisted of Australian, Belgian, Malaysian, Dutch, and Ukrainian investigators, together with the Ukrainian government's own investigation, found that the missile was launched from an agricultural field near Pervomaiskyi—an area controlled by pro-Russian fighters. The JIT's report used witness testimony and satellite imagery to pinpoint a high-ground launch site. They claimed to be able to track the missile trailer from Russia to the launch site and back again, after the plane was shot down. Unfortunately, the JIT was unable to name specific rebel fighters who would have been individually responsible, but they identified a list of around a hundred possible suspects.

However, without the help of the Russian government in investigating and prosecuting these individuals, it's unclear where the JIT could turn with its evidence. It has appealed to witnesses to come forward, offering lower jail terms or immunity from criminal liability for those who cooperate. But that might not make any difference, as Russia denies any involvement and has used its UN Security Council veto to block the creation of an international tribunal to prosecute suspects. Russia's foreign ministry called the JIT investigation "biased and politically motivated."

It would seem MH17 was particularly unlucky. If Russian-backed rebels did mistake it for a Ukrainian Air Force jet, then it's surprising that no more commercial liners were shot down: 160 planes traveled over the region that day, and at the exact time of

STRANGE
SUSPICION

If one of their missile launchers didn't down the plane, what did the Russians say happened? Four days after the crash, Russian military leaders claimed there was a momentary blip on their radar that showed a Ukrainian Su-25 fighter jet within three miles of the plane's location. They claimed the jet had shot down MH17 from the sky. But Western experts were quick to debunk the theory, arguing that the Su-25 is a close-air support aircraft that normally operates just above ground level to attack tanks and other land vehicles. It doesn't have a pressurized cockpit, so isn't designed to fly at the cruising altitude of the Boeing 777-200. A Russian TV station carried out an experiment to prove that the Su-25 could fly at 33,000 feet, but only if it discarded its weapons. However, the

Above: The style of Su-25 fighter jet which Russian military leaders claimed shot at MH17.

plane is much slower than the Boeing, and would never have been able to keep up with it, and the type of heat-seeking missiles it carries wouldn't have caused the deadly damage inflicted on the Malaysia Air plane.

the crash, there were three other commercial airliners flying in the vicinity. As of writing, the families of those who died in the disaster have still not gotten the justice they long for, although some are attempting to sue the Russian government.

SERIAL KILLING

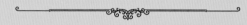

Serial killers are the stuff of horror movies and psychological thrillers: unassuming men who go about their normal business by day only to transform into unhinged sadists by night. They murder prostitutes and couples kissing in the back seats of cars. They leave clues, markers, boasting of their prowess, teasing the public and the police as they desperately try to catch the killer before he claims his next victim. In cinema, and sometimes in real life, the investigators are triumphant, but some of the world's most notorious serial killers—their notoriety heightened by their elusiveness—have never been caught.

This chapter takes you from Victorian East London, where a man who is often regarded as one of the first true serial killers—Jack the Ripper—prowled the streets committing gruesome murders of women, to the suburban homes and roads of California in the sixties, seventies, and eighties, where the unsolved crimes of the Zodiac killer and the Original Night Stalker terrorized families for decades. We find that the reality of an uncaught serial killer is not the thrilling chase depicted on the silver screen, but rather a horrifying game of cat and mouse. In this game, the mouse has murder on his mind, and always gets away, and innocently taking some pain pills for a headache can turn you into the latest victim.

Left: The crimes of Jack the Ripper shocked Victorian London, inspired artworks, and capitvated generations of sleuths.

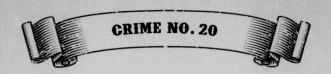

WHAT WAS JACK THE RIPPER'S REAL IDENTITY?

Date: August to November 1888
Location: East London, UK

The Gothic horror of London's real-life bogeyman continues to intrigue historians and tourists. But the nineteenth-century killer's true identity remains hidden to this day.

Of all the murders that took place in the crime-ridden area of Whitechapel, East London, in the last few months of 1888, there are five that are thought to be connected. They bear all the hallmarks of one killer whose identity remains unknown but whose nickname lives on in infamy: Jack the Ripper.

The first murder was that of Mary Ann Nichols. Nichols was a forty-four-year-old mother of five who had separated from her husband in 1881. She had moved from workhouse to workhouse, earning her keep, but was working as a prostitute in the few months before her death. Her body was discovered in a dark alleyway called Buck's Row. Her neck had been slashed and there were several incisions across her abdomen. It was the morning of August 31.

Right: The desolate alleyways of East London where Jack the Ripper's victims were found are hard to imagine in today's cosmopolitan city.

MORE DEATHS IN WHITECHAPEL

Just as police were getting to grips with the events of the previous week—an experienced and respected police officer, Inspector Frederick George Abberline, had just been brought in to take over the case—the killer claimed another victim. On the morning of September 7, the body of forty-seven-year-old Annie Chapman was found less than a mile from where Nichols had died. Chapman had also worked as a prostitute after her husband had passed away. Her death was even more grisly: the killer had slit her throat, and cut out and taken her uterus. There was something else unusual about the murder: next to the body was a freshly washed leather apron. Other sex workers in the area had notified the police about a particular man they referred to as "Leather Apron" because he always wore one, who had been trying to extort them out of their earnings, threatening to cut women open if they didn't acquiesce.

After Chapman's death the police presence in the area was dramatically increased. A group of local businessmen also got together to form the Mile End Vigilance Committee to aid the

PUNCH, OR THE LONDON CHARIVARI.—September 22, 1888.

BLIND-MAN'S BUFF.
(As played by the Police.)
"TURN ROUND THREE TIMES,
AND CATCH WHOM YOU MAY!"

Above: Punch magazine mocks the police force's inability to catch such a prolific killer.

police and to raise reward funds. Initially, it appeared the vigilance of the police and the public had paid off; for a few weeks the killer lay low. Then, on the night of September 30, he struck again—but this time one victim wasn't enough. Two women lost their lives in the space of an hour: forty-five-year-old Elizabeth Stride and forty-six-year-old Catherine Eddowes. Both had their throats cut, but Stride's body had not been mutilated (police believed the killer might have been disturbed). Eddowes, on the other hand, had suffered the same injuries as Nichols and Chapman, but her face had also been mutilated, and her intestines draped over her shoulder.

Even though the police hadn't caught the killer, by mid-November East End life had started to get back to normal. Perhaps Jack the Ripper had had his fill? But on the morning of November 9, it became clear that was wishful thinking. Thomas Bowyer knocked on Mary Jane Kelly's door after being asked by her landlord to collect her rent money. When she didn't answer, and he realized the door was locked, he peered through the curtains only to discover her dead body lying on the bed. Kelly's autopsy relays the severity of her injuries: "the whole of the surface of the abdomen and thighs were removed … the breasts were cut off, the arms mutilated … and the face hacked beyond recognition of the features."

PRIME SUSPECTS

More than five hundred individuals have been suspects in the killings—although most of these are unofficial, given the vast number of theories that arose in the twentieth century. One of the earliest official suspects was "Leather Apron." After Chapman's murder, police arrested John Pizer, who was known by that moniker, but he had solid alibis for the nights of Nichols' and

Chapman's deaths. At the latter's inquest, he was officially cleared of any involvement.

It was concluded that the killer was likely to be a local man after a bloodstained portion of Eddowes' apron was found in a doorway on nearby Goulston Street. It was thought he might have used it to wipe his hands and the murder weapon clean before retreating to his lodgings nearby. Another assumption was that the killer might have been Jewish. A message that read something to the effect of "The Jews are the men that will not be blamed for nothing," was found scribbled in chalk near to where Eddowes was killed, and was thought to be a clue to the killer's identity, although police were quick to remove it for fear of an anti-Semitic backlash.

Above: The *Illustrated London News* published this drawing showing the Mile End Vigiliance Committee in action. It was titled "A Suspicious Character."

One of the more promising leads at the time was Severin Klosowski, a Polish barber who went by the name George Chapman. He had only arrived in London the year the murders began. In 1903, he was charged with poisoning three former partners using antimony, and found guilty of the murder of one of them. Inspector Abberline thought Klosowski was the most likely Ripper suspect. In a statement he said, "I have been so struck with the remarkable coincidences in the two series of murders that I have not been able to think of anything else for several days past … everything fits in and dovetails so well that I cannot help feeling that this is the man we struggled so hard to capture fifteen years ago."

Many believed the Ripper to have had some medical training. In the inquest into Eddowes' murder, Dr. Frederick Gordon Brown,

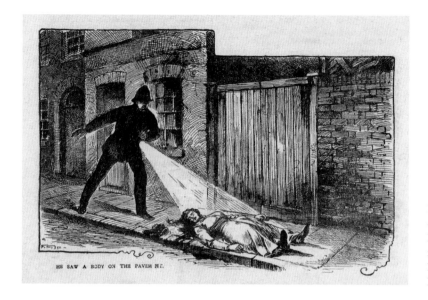

HE SAW A BODY ON THE PAVEMENT.

Left: An illustration depicting the dead body of the Ripper's first victim, Mary Ann Nichols, found on Buck's Row.

the London police surgeon who performed the autopsy, said, "I believe the perpetrator of the act must have had considerable knowledge of the position of the organs in the abdominal cavity and the way of removing them." Two doctors whose names have been bandied about in Ripper theories include Dr. Montague John Druitt, who went missing around the time of Kelly's murder—his own body was found floating in the River Thames a month later—and Dr. Thomas Neill Cream, an abortionist who was found guilty of murdering four women by poisoning them in 1892. As he was hanged for his crimes he reportedly said, "I am Jack," although this is widely disputed, and records show he was in prison at the time of the murders.

Jack the Ripper is ingrained in popular culture. Through the years the name has stood as a warning to children who misbehave and women who dare to walk alone at night. But so many years on, with scant physical evidence to analyze and no definitive leads to go on, the real name behind the grisly murders of that fateful autumn will likely remain a mystery forever.

— STRANGE —
SUSPICION

With the public's appetite for Jack the Ripper theories whetted by the surge in books on the subject in the 1960s, it's not surprising that a number of high-profile men from the period have come under suspicion. From *Alice's Adventures in Wonderland* author Lewis Carroll (real name Charles Dodgson) to renowned twentieth-century artist Walter Sickert, many of these absurd claims have little evidence to support them. The same can be said for the naming of Prince Albert Victor, the Duke of Clarence (one of Queen Victoria's grandchildren). While not a suspect at the time, three separate theories from the sixties onward have placed the prince at the center of the Ripper story. One of them created a sensation when it was published in an article in *The Criminologist* in 1970. The theory, by Dr. Thomas Stowell, was allegedly based on private notes taken by the prince's doctor. It posits that the prince had been compelled

Above: Prince Albert Victor was only regarded as a possible suspect following a series of theories and articles published from the 1960s onward.

to commit the murders after being driven to insanity due to syphilis. The theory has been widely panned because these "notes" have never been publicly examined, and records show that the prince was in Yorkshire, Scotland, and Sandringham on the dates the murders were committed.

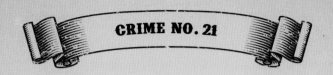

WHO WAS THE AXEMAN OF NEW ORLEANS?

Date: June 1911 to March 1919
Location: New Orleans, Louisiana, USA

For one night in early twentieth-century New Orleans, jazz music blared out from bars and bedrooms across the city—not in celebration, but in fear.

I am not a human being, but a spirit and a demon from the hottest hell. I am what you Orleanians and your foolish police call the Axeman.

These words are believed to have been penned by the Axeman of New Orleans—a fitting pseudonym for a killer (or two killers) who terrorized the Louisianan city in the early 1900s. The quote is taken from a letter that, if authentic, gives a brief insight into the troubled mind of the axe-wielding murderer. The police solved almost all of the fifty-two murders committed in New Orleans in 1910; most were personal, committed by individuals known to their victims. Murders like those the Axeman committed were virtually unheard of. But even if the letter was a hoax, the author got one thing right. In the case of the Axeman, the police were foolish; after all these years the Big Easy is no closer to figuring out who this "demon" was.

The public's awareness of the Axeman didn't ramp up until May 24, 1918, when an Italian immigrant couple, Joseph and Catherine Maggio, were found bloodied and butchered in their bedroom. Their throats had been cut using a straight razor and in the bathtub was the bloody axe that had done the rest of the damage. Their killer had broken into the house while they slept by cutting a panel in the back door. Outside on the sidewalk someone had written a threatening message: "Mrs. Maggio is going to sit up tonight just like Mrs. Toney."

Detectives thought the "Mrs. Toney" referred to was actually Mrs. Schiamba, who together with her husband, Tony, had been the victim of a similarly grizzly attack six years earlier on May 15, 1912. That incident had been the last of a spate of connected crimes during that period, which had seen grocer August Crutti and his wife struck by a meat cleaver by a man demanding their money (they survived) on the night of August 13, 1910; and Joe Davi losing his life after an intruder's brutal cleaver assault on him on June 26, 1911. His pregnant wife, who'd been beside him in bed that night and had been struck across the face, survived to tell the tale. If the 1918–19 killer was a different man, as many people believe

Below: The culture and character of New Orleans was tarnished by a jazz-loving "demon" who terrorized the city in the early 1900s.

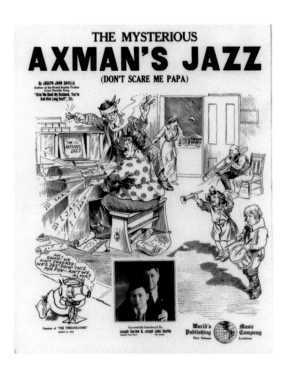

THE MYSTERIOUS
AXMAN'S JAZZ
(DON'T SCARE ME PAPA)

Above: The idea of families playing music to ward off the killer was satirized on the sheet music for Joseph John Davilla's *The Mysterious Axeman's Jazz (Don't Scare Me Papa)*.

he was, his blood lust was less satiable than his predecessor's. On June 28, a month after the Maggios' deaths, a Polish couple, Louis Besumer and Harriet Lowe, were injured in a similar attack. Besumer survived, but Lowe died from her injuries on August 5. That same day, Edward Schneider returned home to find his unconscious wife lying in a pool of her own blood. Fortunately, she survived to tell the tale of an axe-wielding "phantom" who had broken into the house and attacked her. Then, on August 10, 1918, Joseph Romano, an elderly man living with his two nieces, woke to a tall man dressed in a slouch hat and dark suit slashing at him with an axe. He died from two gaping wounds to the head after being rushed to hospital.

THE LETTER

By March 14, 1919, the Axeman had been responsible for six similar home invasions, which had resulted in eight murders and ten victims with serious injuries. In many cases, the attacker had used his victims' own axes or weapons against them, leaving them behind. For those who survived their ordeal, the memories of the mysterious murderer were vague, and the police were no closer to catching him. It was on this date, four days after the latest victim had lost her life, that the *New Orleans Times-Picayune* newspaper received a rather unusual letter, claiming to be from the Axeman. "They have never caught me and they never will," read the letter. The author went on to describe himself as "not a human being, but a spirit and a demon from the hottest hell." It was a warning to the people of New Orleans, who might have thought the ordeal was over.

When I see fit, I shall come and claim other victims. I alone know whom they shall be. I shall leave no clue except my bloody axe, besmeared with blood and brains of he whom I have sent below to keep me company.

The author declared that on the following Tuesday night, he would "pass over New Orleans" and that, being fond of jazz music, he would spare all those whose home blared out the sounds of jazz. Those who didn't would "get the axe." No one faced the Axeman that night, but many people did blast jazz music or go to clubs just in case.

GROCER GRUDGE

In 1919 there were four more Axeman incidents. The last of these was the death of Mike Pepitone, who, on October 27, had his face turned into an "unrecognizable mass" after the perpetrator smashed it in using an iron bar—Pepitone didn't own an axe. Many of the Axeman's victims, including Pepitone, were grocers and members of the city's Italian immigrant community. In the late nineteenth and early twentieth centuries many Italians had been brought to America's Deep South to labor in the cotton fields.

Right: Many of the Axeman's victims were part of the Italian immigrant community and ran corner stores like this one.

But their work ethic, and their commitment to living on very little, soon saw many of them save enough to go into business for themselves, often as fruit and vegetable vendors, leaving behind the poverty suffered by many poor black and white families. By the early 1900s, when the Axeman was terrorizing the city, Italian grocers were dominating the corner store industry. It is widely believed the killer was either a white laborer who was jealous and angry at these newcomers who were doing so well or a vengeful burglar who had been sent to jail after robbing an Italian store.

Of course, the Italian connection has led many to theorize that these were not random home invasions and murders, but deliberate Mafia hits. Perhaps these grocers were refusing to pay Mafia bribes and their deaths were enacted to send a message to others. The city was not host to a sophisticated criminal underworld, but gang crime was rife and vendettas between different Italian groups were usually settled outside of the law, with many immigrants reluctant to go to the police. However, the brutality of the Axeman's killings wasn't in line with the strict Mafia code, most notably the fact that women and children were harmed in some cases, and the use of an axe, instead of a gun or a bomb, was not in keeping with these gangland crimes.

Like the unexplained killing spree of London's Jack the Ripper, the dark days of the Axeman will never be forgotten by New Orleans. Today the jazz-loving demon who stalked the streets at night is as much part of local folklore as his British counterpart. But for the victims and their families who survived these harrowing attacks, it's likely the police's inability to solve the crime and bring them the justice they deserved would have been almost as painful to bear as the injuries they suffered.

STRANGE SUSPICION

Left: Esther Pepitone and Axeman victim Mike Pepitone on their wedding day. A year after Mike's death, Esther shot a man whom she claimed to recognize as her husband's killer.

A year after Mike Pepitone was murdered, his widow, Esther, now living in Los Angeles, shot a man she saw on a sidewalk and then waited for her own arrest. When police picked her up she reportedly said: "He was the axeman; I saw him running from my husband's room." The man she shot, Doc Mumpre, had several aliases, including Leon Manfre and Frank Mumphrey. Over time his identity has become intertwined with a man named Joseph Mumfre, who served a number of prison sentences in New Orleans around the time of the second batch of Axeman killings. It's widely thought these two men could have been the same person, and the timings of Mumfre's prison sentences seem to support this theory. He was released from prison shortly before the 1911 murders, then incarcerated for seven years, only to be released again in 1918 just before the Maggio murders. He left New Orleans for Los Angeles after Pepitone's death. Although there was no direct evidence to link Mumfre to the Axeman murders, Esther was convinced enough to risk her own freedom to see him dead. In her trial she was described as a "hoodlum and a thief" and sentenced to ten years in prison.

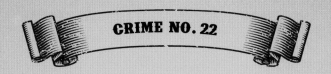

WHO COMMITTED THE CLEVELAND TORSO MURDERS?

Date: 1934–1938
Location: Cleveland, Ohio, USA

Despite the efforts of one of Chicago's finest detectives, this murderous rampage in 1930s Cleveland left a host of unidentified dead bodies and a police force baffled.

There is still some debate around the number of victims whose lives were ended by this particular Cleveland murderer. Some say there were twelve official victims, starting with the discovery of Edward Andrassy's body in September 1935, but an unsolved murder from the previous year might mark the true start of the spree.

The Lady of the Lake, as she became known, was spotted by a carpenter on September 5, 1934. He was taking a walk along the shore of Lake Erie when he came across the remains of a woman's lower torso and thighs, the lower legs amputated at the knees. Her upper torso was later found about 30 miles away. Her head was never found. This was before DNA analysis, so without dental impressions, fingerprints (the torso's arms were missing), or a face

Right: Cleveland as seen from the waters of Lake Erie where the Lady of the Lake, and the body parts of others, were found.

for a family member to recognize, it was very hard for police to identify the victim. A Jane Doe meant there was little information to go on and the investigation soon dried up. Detectives thought the woman had probably been dead for about three months and was in her thirties. Other than the surgical precision with which her body had been cut up, another notable detail was that her skin had a reddish tinge, as if it had been treated with some kind of chemical.

BUTCHER OF KINGSBURY RUN

For many, the beginning of the "Butcher of Kingsbury Run" story starts with the discovery of Andrassy's body just over a year later on September 22. As the name suggests, most of the bodies were found in Kingsbury Run, in what was then a deprived part of Cleveland. The Depression had hit the city pretty hard. Once a thriving industrial center, the 1930s brought mass unemployment and poverty. Shantytowns in areas like Kingsbury Run and the Flats were where the destitute congregated. Food and shelter were scarce, but crime, prostitution, and gambling were rife.

Above: Flo Polillo was one of only a few victims police were able to identify, despite the fact her head was never found.

When Andrassy's body was discovered, his head and genitals were missing. The victim had been described as a "small-time troublemaker," who was involved in pornography and other unsavory business, not dissimilar from many of the area's locals. During the investigation into Andrassy's murder, police found the body of an older man not far from the scene of the crime. He was never identified, but his skin bore the same reddish tinge as the Lady of the Lake. Both men's heads were found buried in shallow graves nearby. And then the bodies kept coming. A few months later, on January 26, 1936, during one of the coldest Midwest winters on record, there was another grim discovery at the back of the White Front Meat Market on Central Avenue. Wrapped in newspaper and carefully packaged inside two baskets were the lower half of a woman's torso, her thighs, a right arm, and a hand. This was all that remained of Flo Polillo, a forty-one-year-old woman who had been convicted of prostitution and illegal liquor sales in the past.

Over the next few years body parts were discovered belonging to eleven other John or Jane Does, along with some other victims who are less widely thought to have been killed by the Butcher. Unlike many serial killers, whose victims fit a certain profile, the Cleveland killer was indiscriminate: the bodies belonged to both men and women of different ages and ethnicities. Some were unidentifiable, and others had no one to identify them, in large part because many of the victims were vagrants with no one to miss them. There was a growing anger at the police, and newly appointed safety director, Eliot Ness, known for enforcing prohibition in Chicago and bringing down famed mob leader Al

Capone, was having no such luck in Cleveland. Something needed to be done. On August 18, 1938, Ness and thirty-five police officers descended on Kingsbury Run, rounding up sixty-three men and searching the deserted shacks. Then they burned the shantytown to the ground.

Maybe Ness's raid had successfully apprehended the killer, or maybe the police presence and destruction of the area put the Butcher off, but either way, the killing stopped. In July 1939, the first proper suspect in the case was arrested. Frank Dolezal was a fifty-two-year-old bricklayer who'd lived with Flo Polillo and knew Edward Andrassy. He "confessed" to Polillo's murder, although it's widely thought that his confession was the result of police brutality and coercion. Before he could stand trial, he was found dead in his cell. The police claimed he had hung himself, but the public and the coroner were suspicious—Dolezal had broken ribs when he died, injuries he had sustained while in custody.

Right: Police pull a wrapped package out of Lake Erie, where a number of the Butcher's victims' body parts were found.

A SUSPECT DOCTOR

There's another name that crops up time and time again in relation to the Cleveland case: Dr. Francis Sweeney, a well-connected surgical resident. He was the cousin of a congressman, with a promising career ahead of him. He was also thought to be Ness's prime suspect in the case, but there was never enough evidence to pin any of the murders on him.

Sweeney was born and raised in the Kingsbury Run area. His mother had died of a stroke when he was nine and his father had suffered from what was described as "psychosis," spending the last years of his life in an asylum. Like his father, Sweeney suffered from mental health problems. A violent alcoholic, according to his wife he had remained in a drunken stupor from 1929 to 1934, when they separated (1934 was also the year the Lady in the Lake was found). In fact, Sweeney's mental health was one of the reasons he was originally excluded as a possible suspect, because he spent much of his time in this period at the Sandusky Soldiers' and Sailors' Home, sobering up and being treated. When one of the victim's legs was found near to the Home, however, the police brought him in for questioning. It's believed he failed a number of polygraph tests, but the evidence wasn't enough to bring a charge against him.

On August 25, 1938, Sweeney had himself committed to a mental hospital, and is thought to have stayed in institutions until his death in 1964. Coincidentally, 1938 was also the year the last Butcher victim was found. Ness, for his part, was convinced of Sweeney's guilt. After 1938 he received incoherent postcards from someone who claimed to be the killer, signed "F. E. Sweeney." Maybe the good doctor was not so good after all.

— STRANGE —
SUSPICION

There are many who think the Butcher simply moved away and carried on killing elsewhere. A letter that could have been from the killer, addressed to the chief of police, was mailed to and printed in the *Cleveland Press* in January 1939. It read:

You can rest easy now, as I have come to sunny California for the winter. I felt bad operating on those people, but science must advance … What did their lives mean in comparison to hundreds of sick and disease-twisted bodies?

The letter implied that the killer was experimenting on the bodies, trying to prove some scientific theory. "They call me mad and a butcher," he wrote, "but the truth will out." Was "the truth" that the killer was a doctor who was now experimenting on bodies in California, or elsewhere? In 1940, three decapitated bodies were found in boxcars near Pittsburgh, Pennsylvania. The removal of body parts with surgical precision was consistent with the Ohio killings.

Above: The Butcher of Cleveland was known for his unusual treatment of his victims' bodies. A 1939 letter to the police suggested he was experimenting on them for scientific advancement.

A spate of similar killings also took place in New Castle, Pennsylvania, between 1921 and 1942. But despite the Cleveland police being brought in to investigate a link, none was found. In 1947 there was a notorious murder in California that bore some of the hallmarks of the Cleveland killer. The victim became known as the Black Dahlia, and the case was never solved. Turn to page 44 to read all about it.

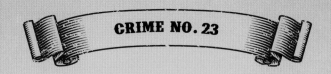

WHO WAS THE ZODIAC KILLER?

Date: December 20, 1968, to October 11, 1969
Location: California, USA

Attacks on young couples caused a media frenzy when the killer started communicating directly with the newspapers, declaring: "This is the Zodiac speaking…"

It was a Friday night in December 1968 when seventeen-year-old David Arthur Faraday picked up his sixteen-year-old girlfriend, Betty Lou Jensen, for their date. After stopping for a Coke, they headed to an isolated gravel strip near to Lake Herman, on the outskirts of Vallejo, California. At 11:15 p.m. a woman who lived nearby came across the parked car. The passenger door was open; Faraday was on his back on the ground lying in a pool of his own blood. Jensen's body was about 30 feet away from the car. They had both been shot. Faraday managed to hang on till the ambulance arrived but died on the way to the hospital; Jensen was declared dead at the scene.

Six months later, on July 4, 1969, Darlene Ferrin and Michael Mageau were parked a few miles away near Blue Rock Springs Park, Vallejo. A man approached their car with a flashlight and then shot at the couple, before returning to shoot them again.

BETTY LOU JENSEN   DAVID FARADAY   DARLENE FERRIN

Right: The Zodiac killer's first three murder victims: (from left to right) Betty Lou Jensen, David Arthur Faraday, and Darlene Ferrin.

A groundskeeper at a nearby golf course heard the shots and the sound of a car driving away. It was Independence Day, so the police assumed the "gunshots" were probably fireworks, and as a result they were slow to respond. When they did arrive, they found both victims still alive—Ferrin died at 12:30 a.m. at the local hospital, while Mageau survived after multiple surgeries. In the car there were nine-millimeter shell casings from what police believed to be a Browning semiautomatic. Mageau would later describe the killer as a young, stocky white male, with light brown curly hair.

THE ZODIAC MAKES CONTACT

Ten minutes after Ferrin died a call was placed to the Vallejo police department. A man told the operator that there had been a double murder and gave precise directions to the scene of the crime. He said that the victims had been shot with a nine-millimeter Luger and that he was responsible, as well as taking credit for killing "those kids last year." With that, he hung up. The call was traced to a payphone near to the Vallejo Sheriff's Office. And there was a witness who had walked by the phone booth and said they saw a stocky man inside who matched Mageau's description. This contact with the police and the public was not a one-off, and the Zodiac killer would earn his name from the bizarre communication that he then initiated.

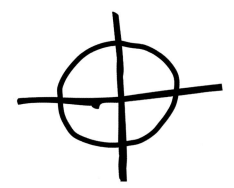

On July 31, 1969, three local newspapers received handwritten versions of the same letter. It began:

Dear Editor
This is the murderer of the
2 teenagers last Christmass [sic]
at Lake Herman + the girl
on the 4th of July near
the golf course in Vallejo.
To prove I killed them I
shall state some facts which
only I + the police know.

Above: The Zodiac symbol that featured on the killer's letters to local newspapers.

These facts were followed by a threat that more attacks would take place if the letter, which also included a cipher the author claimed would reveal his identity, was not printed on the front page. It was signed off with a circle with a cross through it—a crosshairs symbol that the killer would use on all later correspondence, and the brand logo for the Zodiac watch. The newspapers didn't comply, but the *San Francisco Chronicle* did print a part of the letter on the next day's page 4, with a statement from Vallejo Police Chief Jack Stiltz requesting additional proof from the letter writer that they were the killer. A response was received in the form of another letter to the *San Francisco Examiner* on August 4. It began: "This is the Zodiac speaking," and since then the killer has been known by his self-declared alias. The cipher was soon solved by a high-school teacher. It did not reveal the killer's identity as promised, but gave more insight into his state of mind. The decoded text began: "I like killing people because it is so much fun." The killer would go on to send more letters to newspapers into the mid-1970s.

On September 27, some 35 miles north from the Vallejo shootings, Cecelia Ann Shepard and Bryan Hartnell, friends in their twenties, were lying on a picnic blanket enjoying the late afternoon in secluded Lake Berryessa Park in the Napa Valley. Then Cecelia noticed a man coming toward them. When he was quite close, they realized he was holding a gun, had a knife at his waist, and was wearing a hooded mask with a crosshairs symbol sewn onto his chest. The man initially demanded their money and car keys and told Shepard to tie Hartnell up. He then proceeded to stab them multiple times, casually walking away from the scene afterward. Both victims managed to hold on until help arrived—Shepard died the following day, but Hartnell survived. He told the police the man had been stocky with brown hair, and that when he spoke he'd sounded like he was in his twenties.

Above: The original wanted posted for the Zodiac killer. The illustration was based on the witness statements of surviving victims.

The last known victim of the Zodiac killer was a cab driver called Paul Stine. He was killed on October 11, 1969, by a passenger while in San Francisco's Presidio Heights neighborhood. Two witnesses to the murder helped to draw up a composite sketch of the killer, which bore less resemblance to the stocky young man described by Mageau and Hartnell. The famous "WANTED" poster depicted a white male, between thirty-five and forty-five years old, with short brown/reddish hair and glasses. Although the murder didn't fit the Zodiac's pattern, three days later he sent a letter claiming responsibility for it, accompanied by a piece of the victim's bloody shirt and a deeply worrying threat:

> *School children make nice targets, I think I shall wipe out a school bus some morning. Just shoot out the front tire + then pick off the kiddies as they come bouncing out.*

Left: Arthur Leigh Allen, who can be seen here in his driver's license photo, was a prime suspect in the Zodiac case.

PRIME SUSPECT

No one was ever charged with the Zodiac crimes, but years later there is one suspect that stands out: Arthur Leigh Allen. Allen had previously worked as a teacher but was fired after molesting a student in 1968. *San Francisco Chronicle* cartoonist Robert Graysmith, who has written extensively about the murders, was convinced Allen was the killer. For a time, Allen lived with his parents near Vallejo and would drive alone in the area where the Lake Herman and Blue Rock Springs murders took place. On the day of the Lake Berryessa attack Allen had told his family he was going scuba diving there. In 1974, around the time the Zodiac letters stopped, he was convicted of child molestation and served three years in prison. But despite all these suspicious facts—Allen even owned a Zodiac watch—the police had no physical evidence connecting him to the various crime scenes. His fingerprints weren't a match for those found in Paul Stine's taxi, and his DNA didn't match that found on the Zodiac letter stamps. In 1991 police searched Allen's home again after Mageau picked him out from a lineup of old driver's license photographs; they found a

— STRANGE —
SUSPICION

In 2013 a bizarre internet meme began that linked the Zodiac killings to a high-profile Republican politician. Senator Ted Cruz was giving the keynote speech at a conference when @RedPillAmerica tweeted: "Ted Cruz is speaking!! His speech is titled: 'This Is The Zodiac Speaking.'" The hashtag #ZodiacCruz was born, and even serious journalists at newspapers like the *Washington Post* took the time to debunk the rumor—citing Cruz's date of birth (1971), his Canadian childhood, and his love of shotguns and rifles over handguns as reasons he couldn't have committed the murders. Even Cruz's wife, Heidi, felt the need to say: "Well, I've been married to him for fifteen years, and I know pretty well who he is … There's a lot of garbage out there."

Above: Republican politician Ted Cruz became associated with the Zodiac after an unfortunate hashtag went viral.

Despite the tongue-in-cheek nature of lots of the speculation, a poll conducted in 2016 found that 38 percent of voters in Florida believed that Ted Cruz might be the Zodiac killer, with 10 percent saying they were sure he was.

survivalist catalog, live pipe bombs, videos of children screaming, and articles about the Zodiac killer, but no evidence to link him to the crimes. He would remain a suspect until his death from heart failure a year later, at the age of fifty-nine.

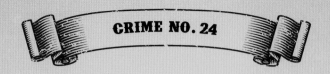

WHAT WAS THE IDENTITY OF THE ORIGINAL NIGHT STALKER?

Date: June 18, 1976, to May 4, 1986
Location: California, USA

Like the Zodiac killer before him and the Night Stalker who followed, this rapist and murderer terrorized Californian communities for years.

Also known as the Golden State Killer, the Original Night Stalker (ONS) refers to an individual who committed a series of violent crimes between 1976 and 1986. His offenses spanned ten Californian counties and resulted in at least twelve murders (of which a number of the victims were raped), forty-five rapes, and more than 120 residential burglaries. His victims ranged between the ages of thirteen and forty-one, both men and women.

Originally known as the East Area Rapist, the ONS stalked his victims, often entering their homes before the attack to disable porch lights, unlock windows, empty bullets from the victims' own guns, and hide shoelaces under cushions to use as ligatures. He broke into the house when the occupants were asleep, wearing a ski mask to obscure his identity and gloves to avoid leaving fingerprint evidence. He would wake his victims by pointing a flashlight in their eyes and, if he'd chosen to attack a couple, demand the woman tied up her partner before tying her up himself. He would tell the couple he was there to rob them, leaving the

Above: An FBI crime scene photo from one of the ONS's attacks. He was known to ransack his victim's houses, often taking personal items like jewelry and souvenir coins.

room to ransack the house, but often only taking items of personal value, such as engraved wedding bands, drivers' licenses, and souvenir coins. Sometimes he would tell the female victim to show him where the money was, then he would tie her up in another room and rape her. In a number of the attacks he would place china dishes on the man's back and tell him that if he heard them fall, he would come back into the room and kill him.

A TASTE FOR MURDER

Initially, Sacramento County police thought they had a rapist and robber on their hands, after a spate of nearly fifty assaults, starting in the summer of 1976 and petering off that same month three years later. The first murder thought to be committed by the ONS occurred on February 2, 1978. A young couple, Brian and Katie Maggiore, were walking their dog in a neighborhood where the East Area Rapist had been active. There was a confrontation and they were chased down and shot. Police later found shoelaces at the scene, tied in the manner of a ligature as had been used on a number of the rape victims.

After the Sacramento and northern California rapes subsided, the violence escalated in the East Bay area. DNA evidence later proved

Above: Composite drawings based on police witness testimony of the East Area Rapist, later known as the Original Night Stalker.

that the rapist had moved south along the Californian coast— and he'd acquired a taste for murder. It was 2:20 a.m. on October 1, 1979, in Goleta, Santa Barbara, when another couple woke to an intruder in the house who quickly bound them at the wrists and ankles. When the attacker went into the kitchen, the woman heard him say, "I'll kill 'em, I'll kill 'em, I'll kill 'em," cheering himself on. She managed to remove the bindings from her feet and escape through the front door, while her boyfriend did the same, making his way into the backyard. That was the last time any of the ONS's victims lived to tell the tale.

After the couple's close escape, there were multiple rapes and homicides in the area. Nearly three months later, Dr. Robert Offerman and his girlfriend, Debra Manning, were found shot dead. There was a turkey carcass left on the patio—the killer had helped himself to the couple's Christmas leftovers. The nylon twine and tennis shoe impressions linked the crime to the East Area Rapist. These killings were soon followed in 1980 by two more brutal double murders and a homicide. The robber/rapist was now a serial killer. Although there were no associated crimes from 1981, his last known murder occurred years later in 1986 in Irvine, California.

Police have not given up hope of catching the ONS. They believe the killer is now between sixty and seventy-five years old. He has consistently been described as a white male, around 6 feet tall, with an athletic build and blond or light brown hair. The killer was proficient with guns and police believe he might have some military training or an interest in law enforcement techniques. The clear DNA profile the perpetrator has left behind means the police

— STRANGE —
SUSPICION

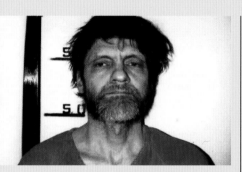

Left: Ted Kaczynski, who became known as the Unabomber after a series of bomb attacks on universities and airlines, was one of thousands of ONS suspects.

Despite pages of eyewitness testimony and plenty of physical evidence, there have been some eight thousand suspects in the case and not one conviction. At one point some people thought the Unabomber, Ted Kaczynski, might have been the ONS because of his resemblance to the composite drawings. (Kaczynski killed three people and injured twenty-three in a series of mailed and hand-delivered bomb attacks between 1978 and 1995.) There was a suspect whose name was never released to the public, who was stopped by police after one of the earlier rapes. He had lube on his front seat and weapons in the trunk of his car, but there wasn't enough evidence to arrest him, although he was never cleared of involvement. Another suspect was Brett Glasby. Glasby was a patient of murder victim Dr. Offerman, and had lived in the vicinity of the earlier rape crimes. Evidence that the ONS had brought a three-toed dog along to some of the attacks made some more suspicious of Glasby, who owned such a pet. However, Glasby was killed in Mexico in 1982, meaning he couldn't have been responsible for the 1986 rape/murder.

are able to eliminate any possible suspects through a simple test. On June 15, 2016, the FBI held a press conference to announce a $50,000 reward for information leading to the arrest and conviction of the killer, in the hope of sparking renewed interest in the case.

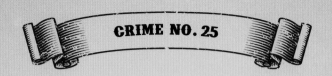
WHO WAS RESPONSIBLE FOR THE CHICAGO TYLENOL MURDERS?

Date: September 29–30, 1982
Location: Chicago, Illinois, USA

A nationwide panic ensued after seven people were murdered in 1980s Chicago. The weapon of choice: innocent-looking pain pills.

Mary Kellerman's mom did what any mother would have done. When her twelve-year-old daughter woke at 6:30 a.m. on September 29, 1982, complaining of a sore throat and a runny nose, she gave her a painkiller. A couple of hours later, the child was dead. Across town in another suburb of Chicago, a twenty-seven-year-old postal worker named Adam Janus had taken a sick day. After picking up his kids from preschool, he said he was going to "take two Tylenol and lie down." He staggered into the kitchen a few minutes later and collapsed. Paramedics arrived but his heart wouldn't resuscitate. He'd died of what was thought to be a massive heart attack. Later that day at Janus's house, in the first throes of grief, his brother, Stanley, asked his brother's wife, Theresa, to get him some Tylenol. They both took some. Stanley died that same day and Theresa two days later.

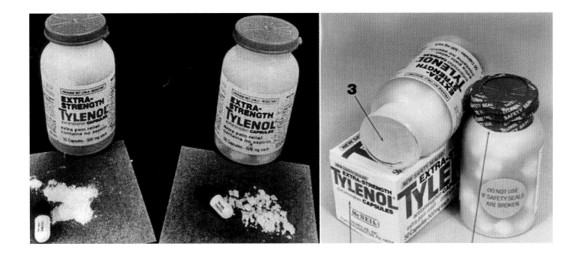

Over a few days, the death toll grew. There was retail assistant Mary McFarland, thirty-one, who was at work and suffering from a headache; flight attendant Paula Prince, thirty-five, who was captured on CCTV buying pain medication from a Walgreens store; and Mary Weiner, twenty-seven, who had just had her fourth baby a week before. All dead, and the one thing these people all had in common? They'd all taken Tylenol shortly before they'd died.

Above: Tylenol's manufacturer, Johnson & Johnson, was quick to act, recalling $100 million worth of products and informing the public about the risks of old packaging.

PAINFUL CONSEQUENCES

Soon after, investigators joined the dots: the connection between them was the cause. The Tylenol pills each victim had taken had been laced with a lethal dose of potassium cyanide. What police believe were thousands of fatal doses had been inserted into capsules and left for unwitting customers to take as pain relief, not knowing that they were actually carrying out their own poisoning. Cyanide prevents red blood cells from picking up oxygen, essentially asphyxiating the victim even if they're surrounded by fresh air. It quickly causes brain damage and cardiac arrest. On October 1 at 11 p.m., Mayor Jane Byrne made a press announcement about Paula Prince's death and told the city that they were going to pull all the Tylenol off the shelves of stores across the city. And by October 4, the Chicago City Council had passed an ordinance requiring tamper-resistant packaging for all pharmaceutical drugs sold in stores.

This was in the days before sealed pill bottles—pills were sold with just a cotton ball under the lid to protect them. Johnson & Johnson, the manufacturer of the pills, quickly established that the cyanide lacing must have occurred after the Tylenol left the factory, because the suspect pills came from different production plants. This meant someone had lifted the bottles from various pharmacies and laced the capsules with poison before returning them to the shelves.

Despite investigating over 1,200 potential leads, and involvement from the FBI and the U.S. Attorney's office, the case came to nothing. One detective thought the murders might have been an act of revenge from a disgruntled Johnson & Johnson worker, after learning of a problem with their talcum powder that might have been caused by a terminated employee, but despite his suspicions, there was no evidence to pin the crime on anyone.

Before the deaths in 1982, Tylenol had 35 percent of the U.S. market share in over-the-counter pain relief. Within a few weeks of the poisonings, this had dropped to just 8 percent. But the company was quick to act. On October 5, it recalled all Tylenol products across the country, valued at more than $100 million. Then they set about developing ironclad production methods and tamper-proof packaging, including the foil seals we know today, which soon became industry standards. Within a year, the once trusted brand had bounced back. The Tylenol name will forever be associated with the Chicago murders, however, because in 1983 U.S. Congress passed the "Tylenol bill" making it a federal offense to tamper with consumer products.

In a 2012 interview about the killings, Tyrone Fahner, the Illinois Attorney General at the time, said: "I don't mean to be

— STRANGE —
SUSPICION

No one has ever been charged with the Tylenol murders, but one man has spent time in prison in relation to the killings. On October 6, an extortion letter arrived at Johnson & Johnson demanding $1 million to "stop the killings," steering the focus of the investigation, and potentially allowing the real killer to go undetected. In December the police apprehended the writer of the letter, tax consultant James Lewis. Lewis had been charged with a 1978 Kansas City murder when police found the remains of one of his former clients in bags in his attic, but he was never convicted. The judge in the case ruled that the police's search of Lewis's home was illegal. He denied committing the Tylenol killings but he was found

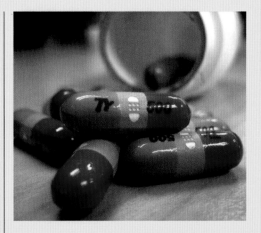

Above: No one has ever been convicted of the murders in which seemingly innocuous pain pills were used to kill.

guilty of extortion and served thirteen years of a twenty-year sentence. He was released in 1995 and is thought to be living on the East Coast.

melodramatic, but it was kind of the first act of terrorism, in that there was no intended victim, just random victims … And that's what terrorism is to me—to frighten or kill indiscriminately." In the same article Jane Byrne remarked: "We did the best we could under the circumstances. But there was a young girl with a headache and she's dead. It was just a terrible thing."

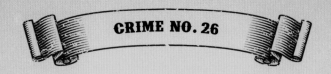

WHY HAVEN'T POLICE CAUGHT THE LONG ISLAND SERIAL KILLER?

Date: ca. 1996 to present
Location: Long Island, New York, USA

When police went looking for a body on the rough, wind-worn shore of Long Island's Gilgo Beach, they got much more than they bargained for.

Shannan Gilbert went missing on the night of May 1, 2010. The twenty-four-year-old had last been seen running from the Oak Beach Association gated neighborhood, a small community of houses off the eastern tip of the Ocean Parkway on Long Island, New York. Gilbert was working as an escort and had spent some of the evening with a client at Oak Beach, before becoming distressed and calling 911 in a panic. According to police reports, over a twenty-three-minute call she told the operator, "They're trying to kill me!" before running out into the street and knocking on residents' doors for help. Two different neighbors called the police, but Gilbert refused to stay put, and the mention of the police seemed to scare her off. What happened next remains a mystery. The police arrived forty-five minutes later, but their search came to nothing. Seven months went by—and then there was a chilling break in the case.

A BODY IS FOUND

Gilbert had long been a missing person—and was presumed dead—when, on December 10, 2010, a K9 police dog on a training exercise made a discovery in the Gilgo Beach area, 3 miles from where she had last been seen. But the body found wasn't Gilbert's. Neither was the next one, nor the

next. Over three days, the bodies of four women were found on Gilgo Beach. These grizzly discoveries were followed in March and April 2011 by the remains of six more people, including an Asian man and a toddler. But still there was no sign of Gilbert. Finally, on December 13, 2011, police discovered her body in an area of marsh next to Oak Beach.

Above: Police combed Gilgo Beach after a body was found—the thick vegetation and rough weather conditions made their job even harder.

Gilbert's disappearance had unintentionally opened a Pandora's box of death. The four murder victims who were found on Gilgo Beach—Maureen Brainard-Barnes, Melissa Barthelemy, Megan Waterman, and Amber Lynn Costello—were all petite, in their twenties, and had been working as escorts just like Gilbert. All of the Gilgo Four, as the women became known, had advertised their services online through Craigslist and Backpage. Some of them had been missing for years. While the different murder methods hinted at the possibility of multiple killers, police were reasonably certain the deaths of the Gilgo Four, who all died by asphyxiation, were connected. Some of the victims were wrapped in burlap sacks, and the close proximity of their bodies—off a quarter-mile stretch of a relatively featureless, 15-mile highway—hinted at a lone perpetrator, now known as the Long Island Serial Killer (LISK), with a preferred dumping ground.

Police were less sure of the connection to the other six victims, some of whom have still not been identified. Although, using DNA analysis, they were able to confirm that one Jane Doe, identified from partial skeletal remains, was the mother of the toddler. This was despite the fact that their remains were found in different locations, and that the mother's torso had been discovered separately nearly fourteen years earlier some 20 miles away.

POLICE PROBLEMS

The Suffolk County Police Department's inability to solve these gruesome murders has been blamed on a number of factors. First, the lack of police presence in the area has likely emboldened the murderer and enabled them to return multiple times while evading suspicion. Second, the police emphasis on the search for Gilbert, who many believe was not a victim of the LISK (see below), may have impacted on the wider investigation. Third, after Gilbert was found, the police department replaced the county police chief with James Burke, who in 2016 was sentenced to forty-six months in prison for the unlawful interrogation and abuse of a suspect in a different case; conspiracy theorists believe Burke may have known and protected the killer. Fourth, the killer's choice of victims is a considerable factor: all were vulnerable women of low social status, who frequently contacted strangers using burner phones, making records hard to trace. And finally, the area where the killer disposed of the bodies was covered in hostile vegetation, which meant it would be difficult for anyone to stumble upon the remains, thus leaving them undiscovered for years.

Shannan Gilbert's disappearance in the area, which is what led investigators to discover the bodies of all these victims, is thought by some to be just an eerie coincidence. Many believe Gilbert's death was a tragic accident, that she wandered into the thick undergrowth, perhaps fell in a ditch, and later drowned. The Suffolk County medical examiner ruled that the cause of death was inconclusive, but in 2016 Gilbert's family hired famed forensic

— STRANGE — SUSPICION

In 2016, more tragedy befell Shannan Gilbert's family when her younger sister, Sarra, who suffers from schizophrenia, stabbed their mother, Mari, to death. Mari had been the primary force in the hunt for her daughter's killer, refusing to believe that Gilbert's death was an unhappy accident. And she had strong opinions about who might have been involved. Mari claimed Dr. Peter Hackett, a local physician who lived in Oak Beach, had called her a few days after Gilbert's disappearance saying he had taken the girl into his house that morning for a brief period to help her and that he ran a home for "wayward girls."

Above: Shannan Gilbert's death sent shockwaves through the small communities living alongside Ocean Parkway.

In 2012, Gilbert's family filed a civil suit against Hackett alleging he had negligently administered medical care and drugs, causing Gilbert's death. The suit is still active, although a judge has dismissed many of the counts. Hackett vehemently denies the accusations.

pathologist Michael Baden to carry out a second autopsy. He was unable to determine how she died, but noted that she had been the victim of some violence. The cause of her death is officially inconclusive, and has never been ruled as a homicide, but it had a huge impact on the families of the LISK victims who were discovered in the wake of her disappearance.

ROBBERY AND FRAUD

There's something truly tantalizing about a diamond heist or the theft of priceless works from a famous gallery. Perhaps it's because these are the impossible crimes: requiring brains more than brawn, masterminded over weeks and months, and committed despite the huge risk of being caught. And perhaps it's because in many ways they are "victimless" crimes, where banks and wealthy businesses, insured against such eventualities, are the prime targets, and where the sheer brazenness of the individuals who pull them off is something to marvel at.

In this section, you'll find some of the most audacious crimes carried out by these daring hustlers. The stolen items—be they priceless artworks from a Swiss gallery, millions in cash from a Brazilian bank, the world's finest diamonds from the French Riviera, or the Irish Crown Jewels, taken from under the nose of their protector from their safe in Dublin Castle—pale in comparison to the meticulous planning and incredible getaways performed by the thieves who took them. They might make it seem like a walk in the park, but carrying out a crime of this nature without getting caught is actually a lot harder than it looks.

Left: This bank vault door might look impenetrable, but nothing is off-limits to some mastermind criminals.

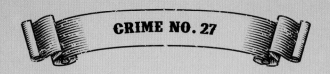

WHO STOLE THE IRISH CROWN JEWELS?

Date: July 6, 1907
Location: Dublin, Ireland

When priceless jewels were taken from the most secure building in Ireland, the scandalous dealings of the order entrusted with their protection were thrust into the limelight.

In 1903 the decision was taken to relocate what were known as the Irish Crown Jewels—the insignia of the Illustrious Order of St. Patrick, a chivalrous order used to honor those in high office in British-ruled Ireland—from a bank vault to Dublin Castle. While each of the twenty-two knights commissioned their own set of badges and star, this special set, worn by the Lord Lieutenant as Grand Master on formal occasions, was presented to the order by King William IV in 1831. The jewels had originally belonged to Queen Charlotte, King William IV's mother. The star was made from four hundred Brazilian diamonds, with eight star points around a shamrock-shaped emerald, embellished with rubies and blue enamel. The badge was similarly decorated.

The rules governing the order decreed that these jewels, along with other members' insignia, should be kept in a steel safe in the newly built strongroom of Dublin Castle's Office of Arms in Bedford Tower.

However, when the room was finished in 1903, it was found that the safe was too large to fit through the door, so instead it was kept in the castle library with the intention of being replaced by a smaller safe in due course. It never was.

The jewels were under the watchful (or not, as it turned out) eye of the Ulster King of Arms, Sir Arthur Vicars. There were only two keys to the safe, and he was responsible for both. The library also had a lockable door, but there were a number of official copies of that key (and possibly some unofficial ones too). The last time the jewels were seen was on June 11, 1907, when Vicars had showed them to the Duke of Northumberland's librarian. Nearly a month later, on the morning of July 6, Mrs. Farrell, the office cleaner, found the keys in the library door, which was ajar. Vicars was informed, but no action was taken. Later that day, at 2:15 p.m., Vicars gave the safe key to a messenger, something he'd never done before, and asked him to deposit the collar of a deceased knight inside. The messenger found the safe door unlocked; the crown jewels, five of the knights' collars, and some diamonds belonging to Vicars' mother were gone.

Above: The Irish Crown Jewels were stolen from Dublin Castle, in the city center.

AN INSIDE JOB

When police arrived they soon realized that the safe had been unlocked with a key. There was no time to waste: four days later King Edward and Queen Alexandra were due to visit Ireland to open the Irish International Exhibition in Herbert Park. There were also plans for the king to invest the newest

knight of the order, but the ceremony traditionally required the crown jewels, so was canceled, much to the king's embarrassment. Relations between the monarchy and the Irish people were tense—this was at a time of growing cultural and political nationalism—and the theft of the jewels was a slap in the face of the British Empire. A joint inquiry by the Dublin Metropolitan Police and Scotland Yard was set up immediately, and photographs of the stolen jewels were circulated around the world. All of Dublin's locksmiths were interviewed—none had duplicated the keys to the safe. All signs pointed to this being an inside job.

Above: King Edward and Queen Alexandra of the United Kingdom were due to visit Ireland four days after the theft.

Vicars insisted that neither he nor his staff were involved. Despite the king's recommendation that he step down from his post, Vicars refused. In January 1908, there was a week-long Viceregal Commission of Investigation into the theft. The commission sat in private and didn't have the power to compel witnesses. Among others, Vicars' secretary, George D. Burtchaell, gave evidence on three occasions and painted a picture of Vicars' casual approach to the handling of the keys, explaining how he regularly showed the jewels off to a wide range of visitors. This account backs up reports that the jewels were removed from the safe during cocktail parties at the castle—apparently, Vicars once woke in a drunken stupor wearing the garlands—as well as the rumors that they were pawned off on occasion to cover Vicars' associates' partying lifestyles, only to be bought back.

Vicars' refusal to give evidence meant the commission became somewhat of a trial in his absence. In the commission's final

DUBLIN METROPOLITAN POLICE.

STOLEN

From a Safe in the Office of Arms,
Dublin Castle, during the past
month, supposed by means of a
false key.

GRAND MASTER'S DIAMOND STAR.

Right: Photographs of the stolen jewels were distributed around the world in an effort to find them.

report, perhaps in an effort to put an end to the embarrassing episode, most of the blame for the loss of the jewels was allocated to Vicars, making him into a scapegoat, rather than investigating fully who might have taken them. It stated: "Sir Arthur Vicars did not exercise due vigilance or proper care as the custodian of the Regalia." On January 30, Vicars found out that his appointment as Ulster King of Arms had been terminated. He retired to County Kerry and in 1921 was shot dead by a local IRA unit.

SCANDALOUS SUSPECT

While Vicars' carelessness was no doubt to blame in part, the jewels were never recovered. One of the police officers who gave evidence during the commission was Chief Inspector Kane. He believed the theft had been carried out by an insider, prior to July 5. He thought the open office doors had been a setup by the thief to initiate the investigation, and he testified that Vicars and Francis Bennett Goldney, a deputy under Vicars, had told him they thought Francis Shackleton, Vicars' second in command, was responsible, although he found no evidence to support their claims. Shackleton lived in the same house as Vicars and was known to be always in need of money to fund his lifestyle. There were

Above: Ulster King of Arms Sir Arthur Vicars, dressed in full regalia before he was removed from his post.

rumors Shackleton had organized alcohol-fueled orgies at the castle. Some believe he was blackmailed about his sexuality and needed the jewels to pay off an extortionist.

A 1968 article in the *Irish Times* led with the theory that Shackleton had worked in cahoots with Captain Richard Gorges, a disreputable associate of his. It's thought that Shackleton stole Vicars' keys to make a copy, and that Gorges removed the jewels and put everything back as it was. Other sources say that years later Gorges verified the story; he believed Shackleton had disposed of the jewels in Amsterdam. But unlike Vicars, Shackleton did attend the inquiry. He admitted his temporary financial difficulties, but was considered a "perfectly truthful and candid witness." When asked if he had taken the jewels he said: "I did not take them; I know nothing of their disappearance; I have no suspicion of anybody." The commission found no evidence to support the suggestion either.

Arguably, Shackleton's alleged lifestyle as a gay man, and the "gay network" believed to be associated with the castle, would have been shocking for the day. Not to mention the royal family's association with it—Shackleton had personal associations with the Duke of Argyle, King Edward's brother-in-law. It's thought by some that these factors might have impacted the fullness of the investigation. The king reportedly declared: "I will not have a scandal. I will not have mud stirred up and thrown about—the matter must be dropped." After the theft, it's thought the jewels were likely broken up into less recognizable pieces and sold. The original £1,000 reward offered for their safe return has never been claimed.

— STRANGE —
SUSPICION

Francis Bennett Goldney was quick to point the finger at Shackleton, but was that because he had a secret of his own? The upstanding Englishman had been appointed Athlone Pursuivant, a junior Officer at Arms position at Dublin Castle, five months before the theft. Although he would have had less opportunity to get close to Vicars to steal the keys, and he was not in Ireland in the couple of months leading up to the theft, this doesn't rule out the possibility that he was involved in the organization of the crime or that he committed it on the day. And here's why. After his untimely death from a motoring accident in France in 1918, a treasure trove of stolen items was found in his home. They included ancient documents from the city of Canterbury, two communion cups from Canterbury

Above: Francis Bennett Goldney in his army uniform—he served as a military attaché before his death during World War One.

Cathedral, and one of the Duke of Bedford's paintings. This gentleman was a thief.

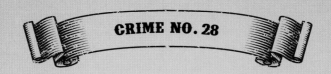

CRIME NO. 28

WHO WAS THE MYSTERY MAN WITH 21 FACES?

Date: March 18, 1984, to August 1985
Location: Japan

In the 1980s a kidnapping and extortion group with a penchant for food manufacturers wreaked havoc on the relatively crime-free society of Japan.

It started with a kidnapping. At 9 p.m. on March 18, 1984, two masked and armed intruders broke into Katsuhisa Ezaki's home outside Kobe, Japan. They cut the phone lines, tied up his wife and daughter, and took him to a warehouse building. Then they made their demands: 1 billion yen ($4.3 million) and 100 kilograms (220 pounds) of gold. They hadn't kidnapped just anyone. Ezaki was the CEO of Glico, a $540-million-per-year corporation and candy manufacturer, known around the world for their Pocky pretzel sticks. But three days later, before the company had paid the ransom, Ezaki escaped. The story was big news in Japan and shocking in a country where violent break-ins were rare and kidnapping even more so. Ezaki and the police were clueless as to who had committed the crime.

The threatening behavior toward Glico continued on April 10 when two fires were started outside the company's manufacturing plants.

A month later, the food manufacturer received a threatening letter taped to a bottle of hydrochloric acid. It stated that the sender had poisoned packs of Glico candies with cyanide, and more letters, threatening to release the candies on to shop shelves, soon followed. They were signed Kaijin 21-Menso, which translates as "The Mystery Man with 21 Faces" or "The Monster with 21 Faces"—possibly a reference to a popular detective novel series. Glico pulled their products en masse at a cost to the company of $20 million. But the police once again came up short. The Mystery Man's words taunted them:

Dear stupid police officers. Don't lie. All crimes begin with a lie as we say in Japan. Don't you know that? ... You seem to be at a loss. So why not let us help you?

Above: Glico CEO Katsuhisa Ezaki, who was kidnapped from his Kobe home by extortionists, addressing reporters.

Although no evidence of poisoned products was found, someone had it in for Glico. The police's only evidence was a blurry videotape of an unidentified man placing Glico chocolates on store shelves (he did not work in the store). The footage was made public and there was a mass panic, while candy sales continued to plummet. But almost as quickly as the threats against Glico had begun, they ceased; with a letter on June 26 stating: "We forgive Glico!" The threatening behavior wasn't over yet, however.

THE MYSTERY MAN MOVES ON

The Mystery Man had moved on to other food manufacturers, and that summer Morinaga and Co. started to receive extortion letters at its headquarters in Tokyo. The letter-writer warned that they would take action if the company refused to pay them $410,000. The fact that at least two people had been involved in Ezaki's kidnapping, and the plural voice of the letters, led police to

Above: Japanese corner stores found themselves at the heart of the story when boxes of poisoned products were distributed around central Japan.

think a crime syndicate was involved. Threats were also made against Marudai Ham and House Foods Corporation.

In October, Japanese newspapers received letters claiming that twenty packs of cyanide-tainted Morinaga candies and cookies had been placed on supermarket shelves around central Japan. This was no empty threat. Luckily, police were able to track down all of the poisoned products and remove them from stores before anyone was harmed. Interestingly, all of the boxes had typed labels warning of the toxic contents, making them easy to identify—maybe the Mystery Man group didn't really want people to die. They just wanted their money. But the letter-writer cautioned that next time they wouldn't include the warning labels.

Police thought the extortion cases had to be linked. The letters had been written using a panwriter, a sophisticated typewriter that is very hard to trace, and one of the poisoned Morinaga candy packets had been found just 35 yards from Ezaki's home. The group initially seemed intent on harming only the Glico reputation, but now they were hungry for money and seemed willing to go to extreme lengths to get it. By December 1984, the investigation had seen two sting operations fail to catch the culprits. It was around this time that police apprehended Manabu Miyazaki—a former Glico whistleblower. An audio recording of Manabu that was similarly worded to the threatening letters, and the fact Manabu's father was part of the Japanese mafia, the Yakuza, gave police hope. But Manabu had a solid alibi, and they were forced to release him.

— STRANGE —
SUSPICION

In 2014, *Japan Times* reported that a man was arrested in Osaka in connection with a series of threats demanding 50 million yen from Glico. He appeared to be in his forties, although his name was not given and the police were quick to clarify he had nothing to do with the 1980s threats. However, he had identified himself in letters as "The Mystery Man No. 28." He wrote: "It has taken some 30 years since the last incident. I have run out of money so I'd like to request some more." Had the Mystery Man passed down his methods to a younger

Above: The work of the Mystery Man continues to inspire—Glico received another series of threats as recently as 2014.

apprentice? Or was this simply a copycat, in awe of one of Japan's most infamous unsolved cases?

The last Mystery Man letter was sent in August 1985 after Prefecture Police Superintendent Yamamoto, under pressure to solve the case, killed himself. "Don't let bad guys like us get away with it," read the letter. "Yamamoto died like a man. So we offer our condolences. We've decided to forget about torturing food manufacturers." While never solved, the statute of limitations ran out on the crime in 1995, meaning the case is officially closed, and even if the Mystery Man was caught today, he, or they, couldn't be prosecuted.

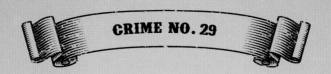

WHO ROBBED THE ISABELLA STEWART GARDNER MUSEUM?

Date: March 18, 1990
Location: Boston, Massachusetts, USA

It was the middle of the night at a Boston museum in 1990 when two cops came knocking on the door. Surely there would be no harm in letting them in?

It was 1:20 a.m. on March 18, 1990, when Richard Abath, the twenty-three-year-old night watchman at Boston's Isabella Stewart Gardner Museum, received a couple of unexpected visitors. The security guard greeted two men in police uniforms, who said they were responding to a disturbance call. Against protocol, he let them inside. They then told him to come around from behind the security desk (where the panic button was located) as they had recognized him and there was a warrant out for his arrest. They told him to summon his co-worker, the only other guard on duty, which he did. When his colleague arrived, the "police officers" put both men in cuffs and marched them down to the basement where they handcuffed them to pipes and bound their heads with duct tape. They then proceeded to rob the museum.

TORN FROM THEIR FRAMES

The entire theft took just shy of 90 minutes. In that time the two men stole thirteen works of art—all but one of which were located on the second floor of the three-story museum. They slashed the paintings from their heavy gilded frames. And while they did steal some extremely valuable works, their choices were illogical; a relatively low-value Chinese vase was stolen, but a priceless Michelangelo drawing and the museum's most valuable painting, by Titian, were not. They made off with three Rembrandts, works by Flinck, Manet, and Degas, and Vermeer's *The Concert*, arguably the most valuable of all the stolen works.

Above: *The Concert* (1664), by Dutch painter Johannes Vermeer, was possibly the most valuable work stolen in the theft, with an estimated value of $200 million.

The next morning, when the security guard arrived to relieve his colleagues, he discovered the robbery and notified police. Very quickly, the FBI seized control of the investigation, based on the likelihood that the paintings would have crossed state lines. But many feel that shutting out local law enforcement was a big error, as much of the evidence gathered since has pointed to the involvement of local Boston gangs. It would be four years before a significant lead emerged.

In 1994 the museum's director received a letter that promised the return of all the stolen works in exchange for $2.6 million. If the museum was interested, the letter said, then the *Boston Globe* newspaper was to display the number "1" prominently in a business story. At the museum's request, the paper did so, but the writer of the letter never made contact again. Perhaps it was a hoax, or perhaps they got spooked when they learned the police had been contacted.

Left: Was the robbery of the Isabella Stewart Gardner Musuem in Boston, Massachusetts, an inside job?

There were some suspicions that this was an inside job. Why did Abath ignore protocol and then move away from the museum's only security system? He claimed he believed they were real cops and did as he was told to avoid getting arrested—he had tickets to a rock concert that he didn't want to miss. Abath was a music school dropout with a fondness for marijuana, and he often showed up to work drunk, but was he an art thief? Motion sensors picked up the thieves' steps as they made their way through the museum, but they never entered the first-floor gallery from where Manet's *Chez Tortoni* was stolen. Also, Abath had briefly opened the side door of the museum before he buzzed the thieves in at that same entrance. Was he prepping the theft and waiting for his accomplices, or was this all coincidence? And then there was a museum security video, released in 2015, which showed Abath talking with an unidentified man the night before the robbery. Whether complicit or just naive, Abath has always maintained his innocence, but was told by a federal investigator that he has never been eliminated as a suspect.

ART AND THE MOB

In March 2013, twenty-three years after the theft, the FBI announced that they had identified two prime suspects in the case—thieves who belonged to a criminal organization based in New England and the Mid-Atlantic states. They explained that ten years previously, they had traced the journey of the paintings to Connecticut and then on to Philadelphia, where the trail had gone cold. But in 2015, the Bureau announced that the two men they suspected were dead, so they will never be able to prove their theory.

Above: In the Dutch Room of the museum, an empty frame awaits the return of Rembrandt's *The Storm on the Sea of Galilee.*

They weren't the only people associated with the case to have passed away in the years since. Carmello Merlino, who owned a repair shop in the Dorchester neighborhood of Boston, is widely thought to have known the suspects and even the whereabouts of the paintings. Merlino was a mob associate, and had bragged to two FBI informants that he had plans to recover the artworks and return them to the museum to claim the reward money, which in 1997 increased from $1 million to $5 million. He never had a chance to follow through on his claims, though, because in 1999 he was caught in an FBI sting trying to rob an armored car depot. The FBI offered him leniency in exchange for information about the museum robbery, but he claimed to know nothing and died in prison in 2005.

It's thought Merlino's mob associates David Turner (who was convicted with Merlino, and is currently in prison), George Reissfelder, and Leonard DiMuzio were all involved, but with Turner refusing to talk and Reissfelder and DiMuzio both dead, the police had to look elsewhere. And they found themselves staring at Robert Gentile. Gentile is an eighty-year-old Connecticut mobster who has been tied to the Isabella Gardner theft since 2010, when the widow of a convicted bank robber told

Left: FBI agents searching Robert Gentile's home in 2012. They found police uniforms and a handwritten list of the stolen paintings.

the FBI that her husband had given two of the stolen paintings to Gentile. Since that time, Gentile has spent most of his time in prison following convictions and arrests for drug and gun charges. When his home was searched in 2012, the FBI found a handwritten list of the stolen works and police uniforms. In 2017 he reluctantly pleaded guilty to weapons charges relating to a sting operation, conducted by the FBI in an effort to get him to reveal the paintings' whereabouts. He had been secretly recorded telling an undercover agent that he had access to two of the paintings and could sell them for $500,000 each. But with his health failing, and showing no sign of giving up any new information, it's possible Gentile will take the truth to his grave.

In 2017 the Isabella Stewart Gardner Museum doubled the reward money for information leading to the return of the thirteen works. The offer of $10 million will expire on December 31, 2017. A quirk in Gardner's will stipulated that the art should remain displayed in the way it was during her lifetime, meaning no new works can be hung. The gallery has chosen to leave the empty frames on the museum's walls, "as symbols of hope, awaiting their paintings' return."

— STRANGE —
SUSPICION

For many in the art world, there was a clear correlation between the 1990 Gardner heist and a botched 1980 robbery of the Hyde Collection in Glens Falls, New York. The Hyde is known as the "mini Gardner" because of similarities between the two: both collections are housed in pastiche fifteenth-century Italian palazzos and contain works by the Old Masters. Brian McDevitt and his accomplice Michael Morey were convicted of unlawful imprisonment and attempted grand larceny after they dressed as Federal Express employees and hijacked one of the company's vans. They tied up the driver and had handcuffs and duct tape ready to bind and gag prisoners once inside the museum. But the plan failed after they got stuck in traffic and arrived at the Hyde Collection after it had closed. They were later identified by the Federal Express driver and confessed.

At the time of the Gardner robbery McDevitt was living in the Beacon Hill area of Boston—a fifteen-minute drive

Above: The Hyde, known as the mini Gardner, was the scene of a botched robbery in 1980— were the two crimes connected?

from the museum—although he had an alibi for the night of the heist. Shortly after the Gardner robbery, McDevitt relocated to California to work as a screenwriter. He was questioned by the FBI about the Gardner case in 1992, but was never arrested. He died in 2004, aged forty-three.

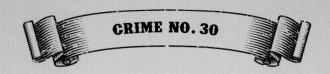

WHO COMMITTED THE AMSTERDAM DIAMOND HEIST?

Date: February 25, 2005
Location: Amsterdam, the Netherlands

In a diamond heist of epic proportions, these crooks didn't break into a jeweler's or bank vault to get the goods. Instead, they took a trip to the airport...

It was just after 10 a.m. on February 25, 2005, that Dutch police got the call that must still haunt them. That morning at Amsterdam's Schiphol Airport, two men dressed as KLM airline workers had made their way into the cargo terminal driving a stolen KLM car. Still posing as airline staff, they intercepted an armored KLM security truck, which was making its way to a Tulip Air plane bound for Antwerp. Armed with guns, they forced the truck driver and passenger to get out and lie on the ground. Then they took off in the truck.

This was no chance hijacking; the men knew exactly what they were looking for and what they would find inside the vehicle. The truck was carrying an estimated $118 million in uncut diamonds, making it the largest jewel robbery ever recorded. The diamonds

were being transported back from a jewelry fair in Austin, Texas, and belonged to a number of different companies. Antwerp, the plane's intended destination, is the world's capital for diamond cutting. It's estimated that 80 percent of rough diamonds and 50 percent of polished diamonds pass through the city.

The men drove a few miles from the airport to the town of Hoofddorp, where witnesses saw the two robbers park the vehicle and get into a red Renault Express van being driven by a third man. They abandoned the truck with some of the contents still inside. Police ascertained that the Renault had been stolen a few days before. It was found a month later in Diemen, not far from Amsterdam. The three men had gotten away scot-free.

Above: A KLM cargo plane on the runway at Amsterdam's Schiphol Airport, where the heist took place.

AIRPORT SECURITY

A full-scale investigation was launched, with twenty-five detectives. The police concentrated on the fact that the robbers must have received inside help. They knew exactly what time to strike that Friday as well as which truck to hijack, and they were able to access a secured freight area, which required a special entry card. KLM was criticized by some for its security protocols in relation to how the jewels were guarded, but the airline felt they had done

all they could. After all, no one was injured and no lives were lost in the heist. However, two weeks before the theft, KLM had been made aware of the security issues with the freight area when a man, believed to be one of the criminals test-running the robbery, stole a KLM vehicle. He wasn't caught, but his description matched that of one of the two men who stole the diamonds.

Above: Some of the diamonds were uncut stones, like these, making it easier for the thieves to sell them.

Some of the diamonds were in the form of cut jewels, but others were uncut. While cut diamonds are usually laser-inscribed, so they can't be passed off to legitimate dealers, and are easily identified if anyone tries to recut them, uncut diamonds are much harder to track, as there are fewer records. The thieves could have easily sold them to a dealer as newly discovered diamonds.

On January 21, 2017, five men and two women were arrested in Amsterdam and in Valencia, Spain, on suspicion of involvement in the heist. On May 3, the five men, aged between forty-two and fifty-five, appeared in court for the first time. They were caught after a vigilant police officer, who was working on a separate investigation, overhead the heist being discussed by the men during an intercepted telephone call. Another one of the suspects admitted he was involved in the heist while talking to an undercover policeman. At the time of writing, one of the suspects is still on the run and the court case is ongoing. Perhaps one of the world's biggest-ever jewelry thefts will finally be solved?

— STRANGE —
SUSPICION

The police reopened the case in 2013, leading to the 2017 arrests. Did that have something to do with another crime that took place in 2013—one that bore a striking resemblance to the Schiphol heist? On February 18, 2013, a plane was waiting on the tarmac at Brussels Airport ready to fly to Zurich, Switzerland. There were twenty-nine passengers on board, and in the cargo hold was $50 million in diamonds and precious metals. Suddenly, two black vehicles, a Mercedes van and an Audi A8 outfitted with flashing blue lights like police vehicles, pulled up to the plane. Eight assailants got out dressed as police officers (they even wore the special security armbands seen on airport security teams). They were heavily armed with machine guns, and held the passengers, crew, and ground staff at gunpoint. They forced security staff to open the cargo door and pulled out the packages of diamonds. The whole episode lasted 20 minutes. The gang had cut holes in and driven through the perimeter fences, and they left the

Above: The runway at Brussels Airport where, in 2013, a heist took place with a remarkable number of similarities to the Amsterdam diamond theft.

same way. Belgian police had more luck catching these crooks, however. In May 2013, thirty-one people were detained in a sweep that saw suspects arrested in Belgium, France, and Switzerland. Millions of dollars' worth of diamonds were recovered. Maybe one of those involved traded information on the Amsterdam heist in exchange for leniency when this case came to court.

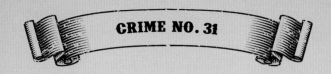

CRIME NO. 31

WHO WAS BEHIND THE BANCO CENTRAL ROBBERY IN FORTALEZA, BRAZIL?

Date: August 6–7, 2005
Location: Fortaleza, Brazil

For months, a merry band of bank robbers beavered away digging a tunnel into a Brazilian bank vault in broad daylight —and no one suspected a thing.

Their cover was ingenious. About three months before a record-breaking bank robbery took place in Brazil, the band of criminals responsible for the crime rented the house at 1071 Rua 25 de Março in downtown Fortaleza. The house was situated just one block away from a tall brown skyscraper in the city's bustling commercial district—one of nine regional offices of the Banco Central do Brasil, the country's principal monetary authority.

To get away with their outrageous plot, the gang had posed as a new gardening business: "*Grama Sintetica*" (Synthetic Grass) read the sign they put up outside the building. They'd gone to quite some lengths to make their cover look legitimate. They had painted the storefront green, taken out advertisements in the local

Right: Inside the "Ritz of tunnels" dug by the criminals right into the Banco Central do Brasil vault in Fortaleza.

press, and were even seen distributing free promotional baseball caps in the community. The fake company was headed by a very visible frontman who went by the name Paulo Sergio de Souza. Described by neighboring business owners as "an affable guy," Sergio de Souza was thought to be around forty years old. "He was a good person," parking lot attendant Chagas Souza told press after the robbery. "He knew everyone here. He said he had come to open a branch in Fortaleza."

When neighbors were later questioned, they said that they had noticed trucks filled with dirt coming and going in the weeks prior to the robbery, but it was a gardening business, so they hadn't thought anything of it. They estimated that the group of men numbered between six and ten (although the police thought as many as thirty-five people were involved in the plot). The dirt was actually the contents of a 260-foot tunnel dug by the team from the house's basement, 13 feet below ground, underneath Duque de Caxias Avenue and up into the bank's vault. This was the Ritz of tunnels. It was built with wooden beams and lined with canvas; it had lighting rigged up and its own air-conditioning system to keep the criminals cool. While the area's sandy soil would've been

Above: The skyscraper in downtown Fortaleza, Brazil, that housed Banco Central—just a block away from the criminals' "synthetic lawn" business.

relatively easy to dig, the team had planned meticulously, and had significant engineering expertise. They avoided underground pipes using maps and GPS systems. And they dug the tunnel during the daytime, so that the traffic noise masked their work. Police estimate the tunnel alone cost around $200,000 to construct.

RECORD-BREAKING BOUNTY

It was the night of Saturday, August 6, by the time the thieves were inside the vault, after drilling through 3 feet of steel-reinforced concrete. The bank was closed over the weekend as normal, but the motion sensors and security cameras didn't detect anything. The robbers must have known there was a lot of money to steal that weekend; a shipment of brand new notes had arrived, ready to be released into circulation, and a stash of old notes that had been withdrawn was waiting to be assessed. The thieves went straight for the used notes: five large containers of 50-real bills. In total the money weighed 3.5 metric tons. To put it into perspective, that's the approximate weight of seven fully grown polar bears. The cash was pulled manually through the tunnel using a pulley system. It's thought that retrieving the money would've taken the thieves at least the whole of Sunday. In total, 164.7 million reais were stolen, the equivalent of $69.8 million, making this crime a Guinness World Record-breaker at the time for the most money stolen from a bank.

On Monday morning, bank employees showed up to work as normal and were shocked to find a circular hole in the floor of the vault and empty energy drinks cans scattered about. By then the thieves were long gone; they'd split up into eleven getaway cars and had driven in as many different directions throughout Brazil.

And they'd done pretty well to cover their tracks. They'd coated the house on Rua 25 de Março in a chalky white powder in an attempt to hide their fingerprints. The fact the thieves took the old notes rather than the new ones was no accident either. The bank had kept no record of the old notes' serial numbers, so police were not able to trace the bills. Some saw this as a victimless crime; the notes had been withdrawn and were therefore not taken from private accounts, but from the Brazilian economy.

OUT OF LUCK

Unfortunately for them, the group's plan hadn't been entirely flawless; they'd left behind a few identifying traces. The main pieces of evidence the police had to work with were a single fingerprint, a pre-paid cellphone card, which had been dropped on the floor of the tunnel, and the identity document that had been used to rent the building. The name on the latter was, unsurprisingly, Paulo Sergio de Souza—the affable businessman liked by his neighbors—and there was a picture of him wearing a baseball cap. Then one of the criminals made a major slipup: he bought ten cars in one day, paying in cash. After police found

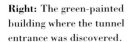

Right: The green-painted building where the tunnel entrance was discovered.

Above: The thieves made off with 3.5 metric tons of these low-value 50-real bills, worth about $16 each.

out, they tracked down the trailer transporting the cars across state lines. Inside three of the vehicles were bundles of 50-real notes.

He might have been caught, but this man wasn't going to shoulder the burden of responsibility. Instead, he sold his compatriots up the river. He revealed that a bank employee had tipped them off to the location of the motion sensors and the fact that the cameras wouldn't record their actions. By November 2005, thirteen people had been arrested and 11 percent of the money recovered. Six of the suspects had been caught red-handed. One of these was career criminal Davi da Silva, who had proved himself to be a bit of a tunneling expert when, in 2001, he'd been involved in the biggest jailbreak in Brazilian history. Along with 107 other men, he had tunneled his way out of the notorious Carandiru prison in São Paulo to escape an eighty-year sentence.

The turncoat's information, combined with evidence from the phone card and fingerprint, meant that in the decade following the crime, twenty-six people ended up with convictions in relation to the heist. Many became known to the press by their catchy nicknames: "Armadillo," "Big Boss," "The German," and "The Tortured" were just some of them. Many of the men arrested were members of Brazil's most powerful mafia organization, the Primeiro Comando da Capital (PCC). The group routinely receives a cut from significant crimes, despite not ordering or organizing the crime itself, so it's likely some of the money ended up in the hands of high-ranking PCC members. Most of the money and the crime's ringleaders, including the boss-like figure of "Paulo Sergio de Souza," have never been found.

— STRANGE —
SUSPICION

Perhaps, though, there were other, more official, parties that received their fair share of the dough. A former bank security guard later admitted his involvement, and it's widely accepted that the bulk of the tunnel-building was funded by the mayor of Boa Viagem, a small town south of Fortaleza. But were the police paid off to turn a blind eye or did they bribe the cons after the fact? The possible involvement of the police came to light two months after the robbery, when drug trafficker Luiz Fernando Ribeiro, one of the heist's financiers, was kidnapped outside a nightclub in São Paulo and his family received a demand for one million reais ($318,000). Whoever kidnapped him must have known that Ribeiro had received a huge sum from the robbers. The family agreed to the kidnappers' demands and handed over the money, but Ribeiro never returned.

Thirteen days later his dead body was found on an isolated road 200 miles west of Rio de Janeiro. He'd been shot

Above: When heist financier and drug trafficker Luiz Fernando Ribeiro was found dead, some signs pointed to police involvement.

seven times and had marks on his wrists consistent with wearing handcuffs. A document signed by state prosecutors at the time the body was found said, "there are indications, not entirely proven, that the authors of the crime are police officers or people linked to them." Later investigations saw two police officers arrested for their alleged involvement in the kidnapping. Maybe the police had known all along that Ribeiro was one of the heist's moneymen. And perhaps they had struck a deal that Ribeiro then backed out of, costing him his money and his life.

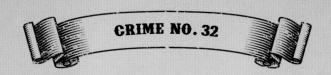

CRIME NO. 32

WHO STOLE FOUR MASTERPIECES FROM A ZURICH ART MUSEUM?

Date: February 10, 2008
Location: Zurich, Switzerland

A quiet Sunday at a world-renowned art gallery descended into mayhem when masked gunmen stormed the building and took off with four valuable works of art.

It was nearly closing time at the Foundation E. G. Bührle Collection in the upmarket Seefeld area of Zurich, Switzerland, when three men wearing ski masks stormed inside and ordered the staff and visitors to lie face down on the floor. They were armed with handguns. While one of the men stayed downstairs, his weapon trained on the terrified hostages, the other two made their way upstairs to the exhibition space and tore four paintings off the walls. As quickly as they'd arrived, the men made their way out of the museum and drove off in a white Opel saloon, the paintings reportedly hanging out the back, leaving a cloud of gravel dust in their wake.

The four paintings they'd made off with were all by nineteenth-century masters: Monet's *Poppy Field near Vétheuil*, Van Gogh's

Blossoming Chestnut Branches, Degas' *Count Lepic and his Daughters*, and Cézanne's *Boy in a Red Vest*. They weren't the four most valuable paintings in the museum, but combined they had an estimated value of $163 million. They were part of a distinguished art collection amassed by famous weapons manufacturer Emil Bührle throughout World War Two and up until his death in 1956.

Above: The world-renowned Foundation E. G. Bührle Collection in Zurich, Switzerland, where the audacious heist took place.

SELLING STOLEN GOODS

The timing shook the art world: less than a week before, a nighttime theft in the nearby town of Pfäffikon had seen two Picassos stolen worth an estimated $4.4 million. Almost immediately, police suspected there might be a link, but all they had to go on was the witnesses' statements saying that one of the men spoke German in a heavy Slavic accent.

While the daytime theft was seen as brazen, it was relatively easy to pull off. The museum didn't have many security measures in place: there were no metal detectors and visitors' bags were not checked. But these paintings were worthless unless the thieves could sell them on, and this is where their plan fell apart. Selling stolen artwork is dangerous and often impossible. The works were immediately listed on the Art Loss Register, making it harder to sell them through a dealer or auction house. This led police to believe that the paintings had been stolen to order, and that the thieves already had a buyer lined up. However, this theory was shaky. The paintings had all been hanging next to each other in the gallery. Had they been stolen intentionally, or were they just the most convenient ones to grab in a rushed job?

Above: *Poppy Field near Vétheuil* (1879) by Claude Monet was one of the four stolen paintings. It was recovered a week later in a Zurich car park.

With a reward of 100,000 Swiss francs for information leading to the paintings' recovery, it wasn't long before two of them showed up. A week after the theft, a parking attendant spotted a white Opel Omega car parked outside Zurich University's psychiatric clinic. On the back seat were the Van Gogh and the Monet. Police believed the robbers had taken advantage of the low-security museum, seeing it as an easy target, but not realizing, perhaps, how hard it would be transport and sell such well-known works. The two abandoned paintings were the largest of the four. But it would be four years before the other two paintings were tracked down. A collaborative effort between Swiss and Serbian police, dubbed Operation Waistcoat, led to a dramatic car chase on the streets of Belgrade in April 2012 and the arrest of four men: three Serbians and a Montenegrin. The Cézanne painting was found concealed in a car (the Degas had been recovered months earlier). Police had discovered a potential buyer was willing to pay 3 million euros, well below market value, for the work. The gang was also found in possession of firearms and over $1 million in cash.

The Serbian police had also recovered two stolen Picassos a year earlier, although no connection has been made public. More and more stolen artwork is being smuggled from Western Europe through Serbia and on to Montenegro, where it's sold for cash to Russian oligarchs. Many of these crimes, including the Bührle heist, have been attributed to the Pink Panthers—a shadowy network of ex-Yugoslavs, many of whom fought in the Serbian Special Forces during the Bosnian War. They are the largest, most successful gang of diamond thieves in the world, and are credited with over 370 heists worth $500 million. But whether they arranged the heist or not, the intended buyer of the Bührle paintings remains unknown.

— STRANGE —
SUSPICION

The robbery aside, the Bührle collection is not without controversy. Many of the paintings were acquired in the lead-up to and during the Second World War—their previous owners were European Jews fleeing persecution from the Nazis. As a munitions manufacturer, Emil Georg Bührle sold weapons to both sides, but maintained relationships with high-ranking Nazi officials. In 1948 an independent tribunal found that seventy-seven artworks in Switzerland had been stolen in wartime France; Bührle was the owner of thirteen of them. Four of these were returned to their owners, and Bührle bought back the remaining nine at market value. But there is still some suspicion about other paintings that remain in the collection, and in more recent years claims have been made in relation to Manet's *La Sultane* and the stolen Monet, which potential heirs claim their relatives sold under duress for unfair prices. Could an ancestor seeking revenge have ordered the theft? Perhaps just one of

Above: Emil Georg Bührle photographed in his gallery in 1954. The Cézanne stolen from the Zurich collection can be seen at the bottom left.

the paintings was the target, with the intention of delivering it back to its rightful owner? The thieves' inability to sell any of the paintings in the years after the heist suggests not, but in the eyes of many, the paintings should have never belonged to Bührle to begin with.

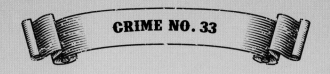

WHO COMMITTED THE CARLTON HOTEL DIAMOND HEIST?

Date: July 28, 2013
Location: Cannes, France

A couple of months after the Cannes Film Festival, a real-life robbery took place on the Côte d'Azur, shocking the locals and putting the movies to shame.

C annes is the crown jewel of the French Riviera, where the rich and reckless go to sip champagne, pose on superyachts, and spend their fortunes. It was also the setting for one of the most audacious diamond thefts in recent years, and the largest ever in France.

It was another sunny morning on the exclusive Promenade de la Croisette, the beachside street that stretches a mile and a half along the seafront. At the luxurious InterContinental Carlton Hotel, where guests include Hollywood stars and Russian millionaires, an exhibition was being set up in a former restaurant overlooking the street. "Extraordinary Diamonds" was a jewelry event put on by the diamond house Leviev, which is owned by Russian–Israeli billionaire Lev Leviev.

Right: The luxurious InterContinental Carlton Hotel on the Promenade de la Croisette in Cannes.

At 11:30 a.m. the exhibition's manager, two employees, and three unarmed security guards were preparing the exhibit, transferring the jewelry from a safe into secure display cases. Suddenly, a man entered the room through one of the hotel's French doors. The glass was not smashed; he'd just walked straight in off the street. Brandishing a semiautomatic handgun, and wearing a baseball cap and scarf to obscure his face, he made his way around the room, threatening the staff. The man had a white messenger bag, and soon picked up a second bag, which he proceeded to fill with jewelry in a heist that lasted no more than a minute. After he was done, he exited the exhibition space through another glass door onto the Rue François Einesy, stumbling and dropping some of the jewels in the process, before disappearing into the summer crowds. The police believe a getaway vehicle was waiting nearby.

The haul included the finest diamonds, emerald and sapphire necklaces, earrings, and rings. In total he made off with an estimated $136 million worth of jewelry. Seventy-two pieces were stolen, of which thirty-four were deemed to be "exceptional." But despite million-dollar rewards, no one has come forward with information leading to the jewels' recovery.

PINK PANTHERS STRIKE AGAIN?

The seafront Carlton Hotel was the perfect setting for such
a crime. It featured in the 1955 Alfred Hitchcock thriller *To
Catch a Thief*, starring Cary Grant as a former jewel thief who
is on the hunt for a copycat burglar responsible for robberies
from hotels along the Riviera. But it was the name of another
film that journalists were quick to mention in relation to the
brazen burglary: *The Pink Panther*. The series of Peter Sellers
films initially centers on the theft of the Pink Panther, the largest
diamond in the world, but in more recent years the moniker has
been more closely associated with a cell-like network of jewel
thieves operating around the world, from London to Tokyo
(see page 182).

The Pink Panthers are believed to have been operating for the
last two decades. Most of the members are from the former
Yugoslavia—Serbian, Bosnian, and Montenegrin war veterans who
were left without a cause when peace came to the Balkans. Their
countries ravaged by war, but with a surplus of guns, they turned
to jewelry theft as a new way to make a living. Although many
have since been caught and are in prison, police estimate as many
as eight hundred men could be part of the wider network. They
are known for their daring robberies around the world. These
include the 2007 heist of the Graff jewelry store in a Dubai mall,
where Pink Panther members drove two Audi cars straight through
the shop's windows, taking off with jewels worth $3.4 million in
less than three minutes; and the 2008 raid of Harry Winston in
Paris, where the four thieves, three disguised as women, posed as
customers and were let into the store, before threatening staff with
a hand grenade and a .357 Magnum. They took off with $105
million in jewels.

The Carlton robbery could have been a Pink Panther hit. The
swift, non-violent, and overconfident nature certainly seems like
their style; though it would be unusual for them to depend on

Right: The glitz and glamor of the Cannes Film Festival brings the rich and famous (and the world's most audacious thieves) to the French Riviera each summer.

one man to enter the building and perform the robbery, and the crime did lack the flashy drama that's become synonymous with the gang's escapades. Interestingly, the robbery occurred just a few days after two Pink Panther gang members escaped from a Swiss prison. Two outside accomplices rammed the Orbe prison gate and overpowered the guards, while jewel thief Milan Poparic and kidnapper Adrian Albrecht climbed over the barbed-wire fence and made their escape. Cannes would have only been a six-hour drive away. At the time, *Museum Security Network* editor Jonathan Sazonoff said: "The theft of high-value diamonds is what they do, so it's not a great leap to assume they are on the warpath again. They are a crime wave waiting to happen."

SCHOOL OF TURIN

But the hotel theft was not the only high-profile burglary to have taken place in Cannes that summer. A few months prior, during the film festival itself, an employee of the Swiss jeweler Chopard had $1.4 million of jewelry stolen. An intruder broke into her room at the Novotel hotel when she was out and ripped the safe from the wall. A week later, as the festival drew to a close, Geneva-based jeweler de Grisogono threw a party and invited the crème

Left: A dazzling array of valuable jewelry was stolen that summer in Cannes.

de la crème of Cannes to marvel at the multimillion-dollar jewelry on display. But it would seem someone was marveling a little too closely, because at 4 a.m., when the jewelers were checking all the pieces to transfer them back to a safe, a necklace worth $2.5 million was missing.

The Chopard thieves were later apprehended (see box opposite), but the de Grisogono case remains unsolved to this day. Some suggest it's more likely to be the work of the School of Turin, a ring of Italian thieves responsible for the 2003 Antwerp Diamond Centre heist. Their long-game approach on that occasion saw them break into 123 safety deposit boxes, stealing 77 million dollars' worth of diamonds, following two years of meticulous planning.

The police have failed to recover any of the Leviev jewelry. Although the bounty was easy to steal, selling it on is another matter. It's likely the jewels would have been divided up, recut, and sold slowly to avoid drawing unwanted attention, making it near impossible for police to track whether a newly crafted piece of jewelry was made using the stolen diamonds. Whether they have been resold back to large jewelers or already adorn the necks of the rich and famous, they're bound to find their way back to Cannes.

—STRANGE—
SUSPICION

Left: Chopard, the renowned Swiss jewelry manufacturer, was one of several jewelers who were targeted by thieves in 2013.

were responsible for a number of thefts and were later jailed for ten, seven, and fourteen years respectively for their roles in the Chopard case. Police in the Carlton case told journalists that the suspect spoke "perfect French" and they believed they were dealing with a native speaker. While Mezzouar would have been in custody at the time of the Carlton heist, it's possible the French-Algerian gang was part of a larger network operating in the region and that the man in the baseball cap was one of the lucky ones who got away. Security experts say the unsophisticated nature of the crime points more to a regional gang or local crime family.

While the Leviev diamond house still doesn't have closure (or their diamonds back), one of the other 2013 Cannes thefts was solved. On June 21, a French-Algerian man named Djelloul Mezzouar was arrested for a robbery at a luxury hotel in Cala Ratjada, Mallorca, and was later linked to the Chopard case in Cannes. Mezzouar, a getaway driver, Samir Guerroum, and a third gang member, Mohamed Marref,

UNEXPLAINED DISAPPEARANCES

When a person is murdered or dies by suicide, and his or her body is found, as tragic as the circumstances are, there is some solace in knowing what happened. For investigators, a dead body provides clues of its own, often leading to the arrest and conviction of the person responsible. But what about when a person just disappears? In some cases, when a person takes off after a crime has been committed—the not-so-lucky Lord Lucan story is a perfect example of this—the police are often left in little doubt that their elusiveness is a sign of their guilt. They simply don't want to be found.

The police's inability to locate other missing people, however, such as New York Supreme Court Judge Joseph Crater or three-year-old Madeleine McCann, often points to an even darker set of circumstances, where a murder may have taken place, but the body has been disposed of so police will never be able to draw conclusions about the case. The absence of a body—whether of a Supreme Court judge like Joseph Crater or a convicted criminal like Teamsters ex-president Jimmy Hoffa—does give people hope that someday the person will be found and the truth brought to light. It also results in hundreds of leads and possible sightings for years afterwards—an amateur sleuth's dream come true.

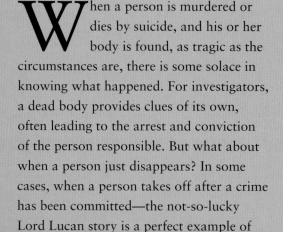

Left: Police search for missing aristocrat Lord Lucan using a Wallis autogiro in England, 1975.

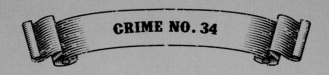

WHAT HAPPENED TO JUDGE CRATER?

Date: August 6, 1930
Location: New York City, USA

He's known as the "missingest man in New York" after vanishing one August evening. Nearly ninety years later, we still don't know what became of the judge that disappeared.

Joseph Crater was a New York Supreme Court judge, appointed by Governor Franklin D. Roosevelt in April 1930. But his career on the bench didn't last long. On August 6, later that year, he vanished and was never seen again. Three days prior he'd been in Belgrade Lakes, Maine, with his wife, Stella, at their summer house. According to Stella, on the morning of August 3 Crater received an urgent phone call. He told her, "I must go back and clear up a few things. I've got to straighten out a few people. But it isn't anything serious, Stell." He promised to head back to Maine by August 6 in time for his wife's birthday on August 9. But Crater never returned to Maine, and his body was never found.

In hindsight, his behavior on the day of his disappearance was unusual. His law clerk told police that in the morning he had destroyed a number of documents and moved some papers to his apartment on Fifth Avenue. He'd also arranged for $5,150 in checks to be cashed (he pocketed the money). This was a significant amount of money: the equivalent of a quarter of his annual salary. He told his secretary emphatically that he was going to spend the afternoon at the Westchester swim club, but he never went there. His whereabouts that afternoon remain a mystery. Were these the actions of a man planning an escape? And if so, where was he escaping to and what was he escaping from?

Above: Judge Joseph Crater—despite his aged appearance, Crater was only forty-one when he disappeared.

But his law clerk and secretary weren't the only ones to see him that day in New York. He'd bought a single ticket to see a Broadway play called *Dancing Partner* at the Belasco Theater, although whether he ever made it to the show is up for debate (the box office confirmed that someone did pick up his ticket). Before curtain-up, he met a friend, William Klein, and a showgirl named Sally Lou Ritz at a Manhattan restaurant. At approximately 9:15 p.m., after the performance would've started, he said his goodbyes and made his way, or so they thought, to the Belasco Theater. The pair originally stated that they saw Crater get into a taxi, although no cab drivers recalled picking him up, but they later said that they hadn't and he had probably walked the half-mile to the theater.

The alarm wasn't officially raised until August 29 when Stella still hadn't heard from her husband, and her birthday, which he'd promised to be back for, had long been and gone (he'd even bought her a gift—a canoe). Stella had sent her chauffeur to the Fifth Avenue apartment on August 9, but it's thought Crater's friends had encouraged her to sit tight as they suspected

Above: The former Tammany Hall headquarters, from where the corrupt organization wielded its power in the years leading up to Crater's disappearance.

he might have gotten himself involved in some career-ending escapade, and they were hoping the situation might resolve itself before it was made public. On August 25 Stella went to the city to check the apartment herself, and found nothing disturbed. All of her husband's possessions were present and in order, with the exception of the suit he had been wearing that night. Even his monogrammed watch and pen, which he loved and normally had on his person, were there. The first news story about the missing judge appeared on September 3, nearly a month after he'd last been officially sighted.

CORRUPTION IN NYC

There were a number of theories about what happened to Judge Crater. Some thought he'd committed suicide or run off with his showgirl girlfriend or another of his mistresses. (He was known to have a number of extra-marital relationships with women in the city—one department store saleswoman, named as Constance Marcus, said they had been having a relationship for seven years.) Some even thought he might have died while with a prostitute, and the whole thing was covered up to protect his wife and his reputation. But most people suspected that he was killed by a hitman, hired by the mob to make sure Crater couldn't spill the beans about political corruption in the city. This was still the semi-official consensus in 1995, according to John Podracky, the then historian for the city's police department. At one point the notorious gangster and bootlegger Jack "Legs" Diamond was thought to be the possible killer—there were rumors he stashed his victims' bodies in the caves and tunnels under his illegal brewery in upstate New York.

And there were certainly some questions surrounding Crater's own financial dealings and his relationship with the powerful Tammany Hall, a political organization that favored the city's poorer, immigrant communities but became known for deep-seated corruption. When he was appointed to the state bench instead of the official Tammany-backed candidate, rumors surfaced that he had paid off the Tammany bosses for his new job. It's thought that this practice was widespread in the city, and that candidates paid around a year's salary to "earn" their new position. As it happens, soon after he was appointed, Crater had withdrawn around $22,500 from his savings and investments, taking the money in thousand-dollar bills. This was the annual salary for a Supreme Court judge at the time. In July 1930, the New York District Attorney (DA) had indicted Tammany district leader Martin Healy for selling judgeships, and if he hadn't been missing at the time, it's likely Crater would've been called before the grand jury to testify. Maybe he had already sold his Tammany friends up the river, or maybe the word on the street was that he would squeal, so someone was paid to make him disappear.

Above: Gangster Jack "Legs" Diamond on the steps of the Rensselaer County Courthouse in 1931. Some think Diamond might have killed Crater.

LOVE, JOE

Judger Crater's disappearance became the talk of the town, and the DA even convened a grand jury to try to ascertain what had happened to him. After taking two thousand pages of testimony the grand jury was dismissed on January 9, 1931, after concluding that, "The evidence is insufficient to warrant any expression of opinion as to whether Crater is alive or dead." Ten days later, Stella Crater found four manila envelopes in their Fifth Avenue apartment, despite the fact police had searched the premises several times. They contained her husband's will, nearly $7,000 in cash, checks, and life insurance policies totaling around $25,000. There was also a three-page note listing all the people who owed him money and when their debts were due. On the bottom a scrawled message is thought to have read: "Am very weary. Love, Joe," or, "I'm very sorry. Love, Joe." Nine years later, with no sign of his return, Stella requested that her husband be declared legally dead. Apparently, every year on August 6, she would visit a bar in Greenwich Village and order two drinks, downing one and saying, "Good luck, Joe, wherever you are."

Judge Crater's disappearance captured the public's imagination. Comedians joked, "Judge Crater, please call your office," and even Groucho Marx made a quip that he was going to "step out and look for Judge Crater." And for a while "pulling a Crater" became a euphemism for disappearing. Over the years, police have handled sixteen thousand leads related to his whereabouts. He was allegedly sighted prospecting for gold in California, sheep-herding in the Pacific Northwest, living as a patient in a Missouri mental institution, and even acting as compère for a bingo game in North Africa. In 1960, with the space race in full swing, the *New York Times* featured a cartoon showing two astronauts being greeted on the moon by a man in a suit. The speech bubble reads: "The name is Crater, Judge Crater." The year 2020 will mark the ninetieth anniversary of his disappearance, and despite his missing persons file, No. 13595, being closed in 1979, as recent developments have shown (see box), the public's appetite for the case hasn't diminished.

— STRANGE —
SUSPICION

In 2005, seventy-five years after he went missing, New York Police received some new evidence in the Judge Crater case. Stella Ferrucci-Good had died on April 2 that year in Bellerose, Queens. She left behind a handwritten letter, found by her granddaughter, Barbara O'Brien. The envelope said: "Do not open until my death." In the letter, the woman claimed that her late husband, Robert Good, an NYPD cop called Charles Burns, and Burns' brother, Frank, were responsible for Crater's death. Frank had been a cab driver, and conspiracy theorists wondered if his was the taxi that Crater's friends had originally said he got into that night. She claimed that the body was buried in Coney Island, Brooklyn, under the boardwalk where the New York Aquarium now sits. The letter was accompanied by newspaper clippings about Crater's disappearance.

Police were able to confirm that an officer by that name had served in the NYPD between 1926 and 1946,

Above: Outside the New York Aquarium on the Coney Island boardwalk—could Crater's body be buried underneath?

and that he would've been assigned to a Coney Island precinct when Judge Crater went missing, but that nothing in their files suggested he might have been a murderer. The New York Aquarium site had been excavated in the 1950s, and while there was some debate about human remains being found there then, police later confirmed that was not the case. There have been no official reports since 2005 regarding the letter or whether investigators are planning on excavating the site.

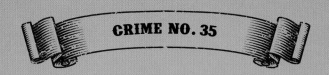

WHAT HAPPENED TO THE ALCATRAZ ESCAPEES?

Date: June 11, 1962
Location: Alcatraz Island, San Francisco, USA

One morning in June 1962, three Alcatraz prisoners seemingly did the impossible and escaped. But did they make it to the mainland and live to tell the tale?

It was their papier-mâché skills that gave them the advantage. When the night guards at Alcatraz Federal Penitentiary did their rounds on the night of June 11, 1962, they'd caught a glimpse of inmates John Anglin, his brother Clarence Anglin, and Frank Morris snoozing in their cells. Or at least they thought they had. What they'd actually seen in the darkness were dummy heads constructed from homemade plaster, made with soap and toilet paper. The prisoners, who had all previously broken out of other facilities, had painted the heads flesh-colored and attached real human hair to complete the illusion, tucking them in before taking off into the night.

At the time, Alcatraz was one of the country's most secure facilities. The prison was renowned for incarcerating problem inmates and escape artists, and housed the most notorious gangsters, from Al Capone to Alvin Karpis. With its island location, a couple of miles from the San Francisco shore, "The Rock," as it was also known, was refortified in 1934 as police forces across the States cracked down on crime. It had tougher iron bars than other prisons, strategically positioned guard towers, and inmates were checked on frequently throughout the day.

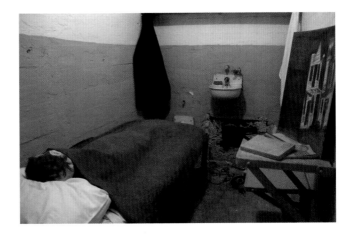

Above: A cell at Alcatraz, which is now a museum, showing Clarence Anglin's homemade head and a hole in the wall where the ventilation unit would have been.

In the three decades following the redesign, before the prison closed for good in 1963, thirty-three other men attempted to get off The Rock—their efforts ending in recapture or death. So when the Anglin brothers and Morris were discovered to be missing that morning, the guards probably thought they'd find them (or their corpses) soon enough. An FBI memo reveals that when they alerted the Bureau's San Francisco office at 7:15 a.m. on June 12, 1962, they were still not sure if the prisoners had escaped. The memo said: "It is not known whether the inmates actually left the island … If it appears that an actual escape occurred, immediate intensive investigation will be instituted." Two FBI agents were sent to Alcatraz to find out more.

THE ESCAPE PLAN

What they discovered was an elaborate breakout that had been planned and engineered over months. In December the previous year, the three prisoners, along with fellow prisoner Allen West— who never made it out and turned informant—went exploring. They'd cobbled together a homemade drill using a vacuum cleaner motor, and used it to cut out the wall surrounding the ventilation unit at the back of their cells. The prisoners had discovered an

unguarded utility corridor behind the cells. They could travel along it and up the plumbing pipework into the roof space above their cellblock. They spent their evenings before the jailbreak in this makeshift workshop, one of them keeping watch, while the others beavered away assembling the various items they'd need for their daring escape.

Special Agent in Charge Frank Price described the inmates' work in preparation for the escape as "fantastic." They were extremely industrious, squirreling away items from around the prison. More than fifty raincoats were stitched together into four life-preserver vests and two rubber rafts (one of which was left behind). They even managed to vulcanize the seams of all these items using hot steam pipes, ensuring they would be as watertight as possible. To inflate the raft they'd made wooden paddles and a bellows-style device out of a concertina.

First, though, they had to make it to the water. On the night of the escape, at 9:37 p.m., West was finishing the hole from his cell with Morris's help. Morris disappeared to fetch one of the Anglin brothers but never returned. By the time West had made his way out of his cell, they were gone. His comrades made their way up 30 feet of pipe work and out through the ventilation system onto the roof of the prison. They shimmied down to the ground using the bakery smoke stack, climbed over a fence, and navigated in the darkness to the northeast shore of the island, where it's believed they launched their raft.

SIGNS OF LIFE

In a series of interviews, West told investigators that the plan had been to row to nearby Angel Island—a distance of just over a mile—and then across Raccoon Strait and into Marin County on the mainland. There, they would commit a burglary to get the clothing, guns, and car they needed to avoid detection, and drive as far away from the Bay area as possible. However, no crimes of this nature were reported over the following days, which was unusual given the high-profile nature of the case. Perhaps the prisoners had help from friends or family, who have remained silent all these years.

Above: The unguarded utility corridor behind the men's cells enabled them to work on their escape plan unnoticed.

Of course, whether their escape was even possible was debated for years. In 2014 a Dutch research group studying the way water moves in river deltas programmed a digital model of San Francisco Bay. Using tide data from the night of the escape, they launched fifty virtual rafts, one every half hour, beginning at 10 p.m. and ending at 4 a.m. They programmed the rafts to travel north, where the informant said the trio would've been headed. The model simulated that if the prisoners had launched their raft at 11:30 p.m., they would've had the best chance of success, landing northeast of the Golden Gate Bridge. But if they'd left sooner than that or much later, they would've been swept out to sea, with little chance of survival.

Left: Alcatraz Island is now part of the U.S. National Parks Service, but its isolated location once made it the most secure prison in the country.

Within two days of their escape, and with no bodies washing up on the shores around the Bay, the only evidence that the three men had made it to the water began to emerge. A packet of the men's letters sealed in rubber was recovered on Angel Island, as was a homemade paddle and bits of rubber tubing. A homemade life vest was also found on Rodeo Beach to the east of Alcatraz. In 1963 a set of bones was found at Point Reyes National Seashore, and for many years police thought they were evidence of the trio's watery end. DNA analysis conducted much later using samples from the Anglin family proved they were not a match for the brothers. Morris has no living relatives to test the bones against.

CASE CLOSED?

The FBI weren't so sure that the escapees had perished, and the men remained potentially at large until the Bureau closed the case on December 31, 1979. The case was turned over to the U.S. Marshals Service, the primary agency in the United States responsible for fugitives. Over the years, deputy U.S. Marshals have investigated thousands of leads. As recently as 2010 an

— STRANGE —
SUSPICION

While the FBI couldn't find evidence to prove the escapees had had outside help from their families, in recent years the Anglin brothers' relatives have claimed that the men definitely made it safely to shore and evaded police, and not only that, but that the brothers were alive and well until at least the mid-1970s. In a History Channel documentary that aired in 2015, the Anglins' nephews came forward with new evidence, which they said they never revealed previously because of the FBI's negative treatment of their family. In the film they showed investigators Christmas cards addressed to the Anglins' mother, signed with Clarence and John Anglin's names. The cards are dated for the three years

Above: Some family members believe the Anglin brothers headed south and ended up in Brazil.

after the escape. They also have a photo which they claim shows the two brothers on a farm in Brazil. The nephews said the photo was given to them by a friend of the Anglins who ran into the brothers in a bar in Rio de Janeiro in the 1970s.

unmarked grave was exhumed after a tip led investigators to believe it could belong to one of the escapees, but it didn't lead to a positive ID. The Anglin brothers would now be in their late eighties and Morris would be ninety, but the Marshals will continue to pursue them until they are arrested, they are positively identified as deceased, or they reach the age of ninety-nine.

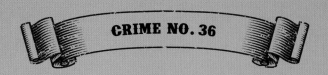
DID LORD LUCAN MURDER THE FAMILY NANNY AND THEN MAKE HIS ESCAPE?

Date: November 7–8, 1974
Location: London, UK

A shocking society scandal rocked London's upmarket Belgravia district in 1974, when a nanny was murdered and the earl thought to have killed her was never heard from again.

Lady Veronica Lucan retired to her bedroom to watch TV with her ten-year-old daughter. At 8:55 p.m., just as *Mastermind* was finishing, the family's nanny, Sandra Rivett, popped her head round the door and asked Veronica if she wanted a cup of tea. After the nine o'clock news had started and Sandra hadn't reappeared, Veronica grew concerned and made her way down the stairs of her Belgravia townhouse to the ground floor. Looking down toward the kitchen basement, she saw that the lights were out, but there was no sign of Sandra. Then she heard a noise coming from the washroom, and before she could react, someone rushed out and hit her over the head four times.

Her assailant shoved his gloved fingers down her throat to stop her from screaming and a scuffle ensued. The man tried to push her

Right: The family home Veronica and "John" lived in together at 46 Lower Belgrave Street, and the scene of Sandra Rivett's murder.

down the basement stairs, but she resisted, damaging the balustrade in the process. He started to strangle her and gouge at her eyes, but she managed to grab his genitals, forcing him to move away. "Please don't kill me, John," she pleaded. Veronica knew her attacker. He was her husband.

Richard John Bingham had led a privileged life. As a peer of the realm he frittered away his allowance on racing boats and became a professional gambler. In 1964, not long after he married Veronica and they moved into their home at 46 Lower Belgrave Street, London, his father passed away, leaving him a substantial inheritance and his new title: the 7th Earl of Lucan. But four years into the marriage, and two children later, the cracks began to show. From the outside, the family had it all—a nice house, expensive things, and holidays abroad. But their lives were ruled by Lord Lucan's gambling, with his behavior becoming increasingly reckless, and the couple weren't happy; Veronica had been entertaining the advances of another man in their social circle, although Lucan soon put a stop to that, causing her to descend into a state of depression.

Left: The car Lord Lucan fled in was found three days after his disappearance in the town of Newhaven on England's south coast.

FAMILY BREAKDOWN

Veronica would later reveal that her husband had taken to abusing her verbally and beating her with a cane. He would even provoke her, creating arguments that he was secretly recording, preparing a case against his wife so he could get custody of the children. It all came to a head in 1973 when Lucan moved out of the family home. A court battle took place in June, and despite the "evidence" he had built against her, Veronica won custody of their three children, on the proviso that she hired a live-in nanny.

Six women had previously held the post of nanny at the Lucan household, but Sandra Rivett was a better fit than the others. She was also separated from her husband, and she was pretty, competent, and good-natured; the two women were on the way to becoming friends. She had been living with Veronica for nine weeks when she offered to make the tea that evening. It should have been her night off, but she had switched the days. When Sandra descended the stairs to the basement, the light wasn't working—the intruder had removed the lightbulb. And then she was attacked, bludgeoned to death with a lead pipe. Her skull was split in six places and she died from bruising to the brain and inhalation of blood. When police found her, her body had been shoved into a mail sack and the floor and walls of the basement kitchen were covered with her blood.

Lord Lucan had lost a lot of money in the custody battle (£20,000) and was now having to support a wife he no longer loved and children he could rarely see. His gambling habit was getting worse and he owed around £60,000. Terrified of what her husband might do next, Veronica had pretended to placate him that night, telling him she would help him hide Sandra's body. He forced her upstairs and told her to lie on the bed and take some sleeping pills. When he went into the bathroom she made a run for it. Fleeing from the house she ran to the pub at the end of the street, where she stormed in screaming, "Help me, help me, help me! I've just escaped from being murdered; he's in the house. He's murdered my nanny!"

A GUILTY MAN

What Lord Lucan did next contributed to his culpability. He fled, driving 42 miles to East Sussex to the home of a friend, Susan Maxwell-Scott, where he spent a few hours. He told her that he'd interrupted an intruder in the house who was attacking his wife and that Veronica had been in a state of shock and wrongly

Below: Despite vast resources, the police hunt for Lord Lucan was fruitless.

Above: The Earl of Lucan and Veronica on their wedding day in 1963. Their marriage was not a happy one.

believed that he was the attacker, so he had panicked and left. The borrowed car he was driving was found abandoned three days later in Newhaven, a port town on England's south coast. Lucan had also posted a letter to a friend, in which he said of his children: "Tell them that you knew me and all I cared about was them." Many regarded this as a suicide note. Maxwell-Scott remains the last person to have officially seen Lord Lucan.

Over the years there have been more than a thousand unofficial sightings, many of them in Botswana. Some theorists believe that after visiting Susan Maxwell-Scott, Lucan took a taxi to a private airfield in Kent, from where he made his way to France. The insistence of his high-society set that he must have killed himself, and their "above the law" lifestyles, led some to think Lucan's friends had helped him escape, paid for plastic surgery to change his appearance, and supported him financially in the years after. In 1975, a Welsh doctor met a stranger in a hotel in Mozambique who confessed to being Lord Lucan; five years later, a contemporary of Lucan's died in a car accident and in his address book it read: "Lord Lucan c/o Hotel Les Ambassadeurs, Beira, Mozambique." It later transpired that the hotel register for 1975 included the name "Maxwell-Scott."

An inquest held in June 1975 found that Lord Lucan was Sandra Rivett's murderer. The police believed that his wife, not Sandra, was the intended target. There are many that think he committed suicide, jumping into the Channel from a ferry. One of his friends, James Wilson, said as recently as 2015: "John Lucan was a gambler. He gambled successfully on killing his wife … but when it went terribly wrong he must have realized he only had two

— STRANGE —
SUSPICION

Veronica remains convinced her husband was her attacker, but what if he'd only orchestrated it, paying a hitman to kill his wife for him? That could explain why Sandra ended up dead instead of Veronica: a hitman wouldn't necessarily have been able to tell them apart. In her book *A Different Class of Murder*, Laura Thompson suggests Lord Lucan arranged the hit but then came to his senses and went to the house to put a stop to it, only to realize it was too late. Sandra's autopsy shows that she was facing her killer at the start of the attack, so Lucan would've known it wasn't his wife if he was the perpetrator. Most of Lucan's friends said in the aftermath that they couldn't imagine him committing such a violent act, but that in a drink-fueled state, and struggling with the custody

Above: Nanny Sandra Rivett was the victim of a brutal attack, but was she killed in a case of mistaken identity?

loss of his kids and his gambling debts, he might have been capable of paying someone else to do the job.

options open to him: hand himself in or kill himself. Having lost the gamble, he chose the latter." In 1999, he was officially declared dead, but it wasn't until 2016 that his death certificate was granted, so his title could finally pass on to his son.

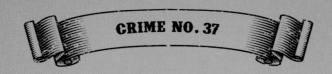

WHY DID JIMMY HOFFA DISAPPEAR?

Date: July 30, 1975
Location: Northwest Detroit, USA

Union leader James Riddle Hoffa lived up to his middle name in the summer of 1975 when he mysteriously disappeared after a meeting with the mob.

At 2:30 p.m. on July 30, 1975, Jimmy Hoffa picked up the payphone at the Machus Red Fox restaurant in the northwest Detroit suburb of Bloomfield Township and called his wife, Josephine. He had driven his green 1974 Pontiac 19 miles from the couple's summer home to have a meeting with two known Mafia figures: Anthony Provenzano and Anthony Giacalone. But, he told his wife, neither of them had shown up. She thought he should hang on a bit longer, so he did. At 2:45 p.m. he was seen by a number of witnesses leaving the restaurant parking lot in the backseat of a maroon car. A truck driver claimed he saw another man in the backseat holding an object covered with a blanket. He was never seen again and his body has never been found.

It's possible sixty-two-year-old Hoffa called his wife because he was nervous. And he had every reason to be. He had once been the

Right: The Machus Red Fox restaurant in northwest Detroit as it appeared in the 1970s when Hoffa went missing.

president of the International Brotherhood of Teamsters, and had been fundamental in organizing the labor union into a national powerhouse with over one million members. But, unfortunately, he had ties to organized crime too, and his influential position meant his activities were under close scrutiny. In 1964, he received a thirteen-year sentence for attempting to bribe a grand juror and misappropriating nearly $2 million in union pension funds, which the Mafia was tapping into to finance its dealings. Despite appealing, he spent four years in prison, until he was pardoned by President Nixon in 1971. When he got out, he wanted his old job back—the Teamsters' presidential elections were coming up in 1976. But the mob preferred his successor, Frank Fitzsimmons, who they knew was easier to manipulate. They'd warned Hoffa to back off, but he hadn't listened. He had gone from working alongside the mob to making enemies of them.

TIES TO THE MOB

Both Provenzano, who was also involved with the Teamsters, and Giacalone were involved with the Mafia. But it would seem they had no intention of meeting with Hoffa at all and every intention of establishing alibis at the time he disappeared: Provenzano was in New Jersey playing cards with his brother, and Giacalone was socializing at the Southfield Athletic Club. This led many to believe

Above: Hoffa's body has never been found. There are some who believe the former New York Giants' football stadium is his final resting place.

the mob put a hit on Hoffa. He knew about their influence over the unions and the pension money being funneled to the Mafia, and he could have gone to the Feds.

The prevailing theory, which was put before the grand jury into Hoffa's disappearance, was that he got into a car with someone he knew, widely believed to be his long-time friend and ex-mobster Frank Sheeran, and that he was driven to a private address, where he was shot. He was then buried somewhere he'd never be found. There are even theorists who believe his body is buried in the former New York Giants' football stadium in New Jersey. But despite numerous digs over the years, one as recently as 2013, the only trace of Hoffa that investigators found was his car, left in the restaurant parking lot, and a single strand of hair in another vehicle they believe he rode in to his death. Because of the lack of DNA technology at the time, it wasn't confirmed as Hoffa's hair until ten years after his disappearance.

But who pulled the trigger? Sheeran has admitted to the killing, and in 2004 even directed a forensic team to the home where he says Hoffa was killed. Traces of blood were found but they didn't match Hoffa's blood type. Mafia hitman Richard Kuklinski also claimed to be the killer in interviews with author Philip Carlo for his book *The Iceman: Confessions of a Mafia Contract Killer*, saying he stabbed Hoffa to death and burned the body in a 55-gallon drum, before dumping it in a junkyard. Another theory points the finger at Mafioso Salvatore Briguglio, a hired gun, and co-conspirators Gabriel Briguglio (Sal's brother) and Thomas Andretta. All three men have always denied any involvement in the case. In 1976, Sal

— STRANGE —
SUSPICION

There are other theories about where Hoffa ended up. One suggests that he wound up in a mafia-owned meat-processing plant in Michigan, and another that he was dumped in a Florida swamp. There was even a story that his body had been put inside a junk car, compacted and then shipped to the Far East as scrap metal. Missing body aside, in 1982 Jimmy Hoffa was officially declared dead. But there are some who still have hope that he made it out of his Mafia misstep in one piece. There were reports shortly after his disappearance that he'd been taken to Gardena, California, as a hostage, but the lead turned cold. And there are always those unexplained sightings from across the border. Even if Hoffa had lived out his days on the

Above: His body was never found, but Hoffa was declared dead in 1982. Was his body compacted in a junkyard and shipped off as scrap metal?

run in South America, it's unlikely he's still alive—he would have turned one hundred in 2013.

Briguglio was indicted for the 1961 murder of another Teamsters leader, Anthony Castellito. On March 21, 1978, two men walked up to Sal Briguglio in Little Italy, New York, and shot him five times in the head. His murder remains unsolved, but it's likely that he was close to revealing what he knew about Castellito's murder, and maybe what happened to Jimmy Hoffa too.

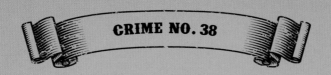

WHAT HAPPENED TO MADELEINE MCCANN?

Date: May 3, 2007
Location: Praia da Luz, Portugal

What started as a perfect family holiday to the Algarve turned into every parent's worst nightmare when a three-year-old girl vanished one night.

In May 2007, doctors Kate and Gerry McCann had taken their children, three-year-old Madeleine and two-year-old twins Sean and Amelie, to Praia da Luz on the Algarve with a group of their friends. During the day there were lots of activities to enjoy at the Ocean Club Complex: kids' clubs for the little ones, swimming in the pool, and tennis for Kate and Gerry. In the evenings the adults would put their kids to bed and dine in the tapas restaurant nearby, checking on them periodically.

On May 3, the fifth day of the trip, they enjoyed the daytime activities as before. But by 6 p.m. the kids were worn out and Kate took them back to the apartment to start their bedtime routine. They were staying in a ground-floor apartment on the edge of the complex, the kids in a twin room (Maddy in one bed and the twins in travel cots) and Kate and Gerry in another. At 7 p.m. Gerry read the children a story and they said goodnight.

Right: The family-friendly resort of Praia da Luz in Portugal, where Maddy McCann went missing.

The room was dark because the shutters were down and the curtains drawn. At 8:30 p.m. the couple left the apartment, the kids fast asleep, and headed to the restaurant 160 feet away to meet their friends, Matt and Rachel Oldfield, Jane Tanner and Russell O'Brien, and three others.

HOLIDAY HORROR

At 9:05 p.m. Gerry went to the apartment. He noticed that the bedroom door was open slightly wider than when they'd left, so he checked on the kids and they were all asleep. At 9:30 p.m. it was Kate's turn to check on the kids, but Matt was going to his apartment (next door to the McCanns'), and he checked on them instead, saying all was fine and quiet. Then, at 10 p.m. Kate did the third check. Once inside the apartment, she noticed that the kids' bedroom door was wide open, but as she went to pull it shut it slammed, as if forced by a draught. When she reopened the door, she had the dreadful realization that Madeleine wasn't in her bed. She wasn't anywhere else in the apartment either. But the bedroom window was open and the shutters were up. Someone had taken her daughter.

The Portuguese police, who have been widely criticized for their handling of the case, spent a year investigating, but to no avail. No physical evidence of Madeleine outside of that room has ever been discovered. Media attention was ferocious—how could a little girl just vanish while on holiday? It was every parent's worst nightmare. But despite the story being broadcast around the world, by July 2008, the police were no closer to figuring out what had happened and the investigation was closed. The McCanns hadn't given up on finding their daughter. After making an appeal to British Prime Minister David Cameron in 2011 for help in their search for Madeleine, the UK's Metropolitan Police were given permission to review the evidence. Everything was analyzed from the beginning, and some new leads emerged.

One of the crucial pieces of evidence focused on by the Portuguese investigators was Kate and Gerry's friend Jane Tanner's description of a man she had seen carrying a child near to the McCanns' apartment when she went to check on her own children, not long after Gerry had checked on Madeleine and the other kids. The Met investigation was able to rule this man out, and it transpired that Tanner had seen a British father picking up his two-year-old daughter from a night crèche near to the complex. Of more interest was a sighting by an Irish family of a man carrying a child heading toward the beach. E-fits (composite images produced by Electronic Facial Identification Technique) from their description were distributed internationally to help police identify if this was a potential suspect. The police also investigated leads relating to a number of sightings of men hanging around the apartment complex in the days and hours leading up to Madeleine's disappearance.

They were not ruling out a premeditated child abduction by a pedophile or human trafficker, but they did learn that there had been a four-fold increase in burglaries in the area during the period the McCanns were staying in Praia da Luz. In the three weeks before she was taken, two incidents had taken place in the very apartment

— STRANGE —
SUSPICION

Four months after Madeleine's disappearance, after a cadaver-detection dog gave a signal in the McCanns' hire car (which they had only picked up twenty-four days after her disappearance), and hair and fibers from the apartment and car were analyzed, the couple were named as formal suspects in the case. The police theory was that they had killed their daughter by accident, perhaps by heavily sedating her so they could enjoy their evening in peace, before hiding the body and faking her abduction. The key evidence was later heavily criticized: sniffer dogs are not as reliable as the Portuguese investigators might have thought, and the DNA evidence that implicated the couple was regarded as inconclusive by the U.K.'s Forensic Science Service (FSS). While the sample taken from the car found fifteen of the

Above: DNA evidence used to implicate the McCanns in Madeleine's disappearance was found to be unreliable.

nineteen components from Madeleine's DNA, those components were not unique to her and might have just been there by chance. Some of them were even a match to the FSS scientists conducting the investigation. Kate and Gerry McCann were officially cleared in July 2008, and have always maintained their innocence.

building she had slept in. Perhaps Madeleine had caught a burglar in the act and, panicking, they had taken her with them instead. Unfortunately, despite more than ten years having passed since that night, Madeleine is still missing. Her body has never been found.

FURTHER READING

Badal, James Jessen. *In the Wake of the Butcher: Cleveland's Torso Murders*. Kent, OH: Kent State University Press, 2001.

Begg, Paul. *Jack the Ripper: The Definitive History*. London: Routledge, 2004.

Bergreen, Laurence. *Capone: The Man and the Era*. New York: Simon and Schuster, 1994.

Bondeson, Jan. *Blood on the Snow: The Killing of Olof Palme*. Ithaca, NY: Cornell University Press, 2005.

Brown, Jake. *Ready to Die*. Phoenix, AZ: Colossus Books, 2004.

Coogan, Tim Pat. *Michael Collins: A Biography*. London: Head of Zeus, 2015.

Cummins, Joseph. *True Crime and Punishment: Heists*. Sydney: Pier 9, Murdoch Books, 2011.

Davis, Miriam. *Axeman of New Orleans: The True Story*. Chicago, IL: Chicago Review Press, 2017.

Dirk, Cameron Gibson. *Serial Murder and Media Circuses*. Westport, CT: Greenwood Publishing, 2006.

Doherty, Jack. *How the Catholic Church Became Naughty*. Parker, CO: Outskirts Press, 2015.

Emsley, John. *The Elements of Murder: A History of Poison*. New York: Oxford University Press, 2005.

Feltus, G. M. *The Unknown Man (A suspicious death at Somerton Beach)*. Greenacres, S. Australia: Gerald Michael Feltus, 2011.

Fleury, John. *Bloody Valentine: The Bloody History of the Saint Valentine's Day Massacre*. North Charleston, SC: CreateSpace, 2013.

Gage, Beverly. *The Day Wall Street Exploded: A Story of America in Its First Age of Terror*. New York: Oxford University Press, 2009.

Gilmore, John. *Severed: The True Story of the Black Dahlia*, 2nd edn. Gardena, CA: Amok Books, 2015.

Hood, Christopher P. *Dealing with Disaster in Japan*. London: Routledge, 2013.

Hoshowsky, Robert J. *Unsolved: True Canadian Cold Cases*. Toronto: Dundurn, 2010.

Katz, Hélèna. *Cold Cases: Famous Unsolved Mysteries, Crimes, and Disappearances in America*. Santa Barbara, CA: ABC-CLIO, 2010.

Kurkjian, Stephen. *Master Thieves*. New York: PublicAffairs, 2015.

Leasor, James. *Who Killed Sir Harry Oakes?* Looe, Cornwall: House of Stratus, 2001.

McArdle, Joseph. *Irish Rogues and Rascals*. Dublin: Gill and Macmillan, 2007.

Meyers, Jeffrey. *Edgar Allan Poe: His Life and Legacy*. New York: Cooper Square Press, 2000.

Miller, Sarah. *The Borden Murders: Lizzie Borden and the Trial of the Century*. New York: Schwartz & Wade Books, 2016.

Newton, Michael. *The Encyclopedia of Unsolved Crimes*, 2nd edn. New York: Checkmark Books, 2009.

Parr, Amanda Jayne. *The True and Complete Story of "Machine Gun" Jack McGurn*. Leicester: Troubador, 2005.

Pineda-Madrid, Nancy. *Suffering and Salvation in Ciudad Juárez*. Minneapolis, MN: Fortress Press, 2011.

Scott, Cathy. *The Killing of Tupac Shakur*, 3rd edn. Las Vegas, NV: Huntington Press, 2015.

Thompson, Laura. *A Different Class of Murder*. London: Head of Zeus, 2014.

Wade Will, Emily. *Archbishop Oscar Romero: The Making of a Martyr*. Eugene, OR: Resource Publications, 2016.

Winslow Gibson, John. *Judge Crater, the Missingest Person*. Indianapolis, IN: Dog Ear Publishing, 2010.

INDEX

A

Abath, Richard 164, 166
Abberline, Inspector George Frederick 117, 119
Ahmed, Mustafa Mahmoud Said 108
Albert Victor, Prince 121
Albrecht, Adrian 187
Alcatraz escapees 198–203
Alkhanov, Alu 84–5
Allen, Arthur Leigh 138
Amsterdam Diamond Heist 170–3
Anderson, Orlando 76, 80
Andrassy, Edward 128, 129–30, 131
Andretta, Thomas 212
Anglin, Clarence 198–200, 203
Anglin, John 198–200, 203
Anselmi, Albert 37
Antommarchi, Dr. François Carlo 14, 15
Arndt, Detective Linda 71
Axeman of New Orleans 122–7

B

Banco Central robbery, Fortaleza, Brazil 174–9
Barker, Captain James 43

Barthelemy, Melissa 149
Benitez, Dr. Michael 21
Bersinger, Betty 45
Besumer, Louis 124
bin Laden, Osama 105–7, 108
Birmingham Pub Bombing 100–3
Black Dahlia Murders 44–9
Bolton, Byron 37
Borden, Abby 22–3
Borden, Andrew 22–3, 27
Borden, Emma 22, 26, 27
Borden, Lizzie 22–7
Bowyer, Thomas 118
Brainard-Barnes, Maureen 149
Briguglio, Gabriel 212
Briguglio, Salvatore 212–13
Brinvilliers, Madame de 15
Brown, Dr. Frederick Gordon 119–20
Brussels Airport heist 173
Bührle, Emil 181, 183
Bundesen, Dr. Herman 35, 36, 39
Burke, Fred "Killer" 37
Burke, James 150
Burns, Charles and Frank 197
Burtchaell, George D. 156
Bushnell, Prudence 105, 108
Byrne, Jane 145–6

C

Calò, Pippo 58
Calvi, Clara 56
Calvi, Roberto 54–59
Capone, Al 34–9
Carboni, Flavio 56–7, 58
Carlton Hotel diamond heist 184–9
Carroll, Lewis 121
Carter, Jimmy 53
Castellito, Anthony 213
Chaika, Yury 85
Chapman, Annie 117
Charles X 15
Chechens 82, 84–5, 87
Chicago Tylenol Murders 144–7
Chopard 187, 188, 189
Christie, Harold 40, 42
Ciudad Juárez murders 66–9
Clemm, Rev. W. T. D. 18
Cleveland Torso Murders 128–33
Clinton, Bill 106, 109
Collins, Michael 28–33
Combs, Sean "Puffy" (Puff Daddy) 79–80
Conway, Kieran 102
Coogan, Tim Pat 31
Costello, Amber Lynn 149
Crater, Joseph 192–7
Crater, Stella 192, 193–4, 195

Cream, Dr. Thomas Neill 120
Crutti, August 123
Cruz, Ted 139

D

Da Silva, Davi 178
D'Aubuisson, Major Roberto 51, 53
Davi, Joe 123
Davis, Duane Keith 80
de Grisogono 187–8
de Souza, Paulo Sergio 175, 177, 178
Deasy, Liam 31
Di Carlo, Francesco "Frankie the Strangler" 58
Diamond, Jack "Legs" 194
DiMuzio, Leonard 167
Diotallevi, Ernesto 58
Dolezal, Frank 131
Drucci, Vincent "Schemer" 39
Druitt, Dr. Montague John 120

E

Eddowes, Catherine 118, 119
Edward VII, King 155–6
Evans, Faith 79, 80
Ezaki, Katsuhisa 160–1

F

Fahner, Tyrone 146–7
Faraday, David Arthur 134
Ferrin, Darlene 134–5
Ferrucci-Good, Stella 197
Fitzsimmons, Frank 211

Foundation E.G. Bührle Collection, Zurich 180–3
Fouse, Wardell "Poochie" 81
Francisco, Frank 99

G

Galleani, Luigi 98
Garay, Amado 52
García, Elizabeth Castro 67–8, 69
Gelli, Licio 59
Gentile, Robert 167–8
Giacalone, Anthony 210, 211
Gilbert, Mari 151
Gilbert, Shannan 148–51
Gilgo Four 149–50
Glasby, Brett 143
Glico 160–1, 162, 163
Goldney, Francis Bennett 157, 159
Good, Robert 197
Gorges, Captain Richard 158
Graysmith, Robert 138
Grijalva, Oscar Maynez 66
Griswold, Rufus 18
Guardado, Jesús Manuel 69
Guerroum, Samir 189
Gunnarsson, Viktor 62
Gusenberg, Frank 35–6

H

Hackett, Dr. Peter 151
al-Hage, Wadih 107
Hales, Tom 31
Hansen, Harry 45
Hartnell, Bryan 136–7
Healy, Martin 195

Helgoth, Michael 75
Heyer, Adam 36
Hodel, George 49
Hodel, Steve 49
Hoffa, Jimmy 210–13
Hunt, Louise 103
Hyde Collection, Glens Falls 169

I

Irish Crown Jewels 154–9
Isabella Stewart Gardner Museum 164–9

J

Jack the Ripper 116–20
Janus, Addam 144
Janus, Stanley 144
Janus, Theresa 144
Jennings, A. V. 25–6
Jensen, Betty Lou 134
John Paul II, Pope 59
Joyce, Junius 95
Joyce, Thomas 95

K

Kachellek, Albert 36
Kaczynski, Ted 143
Kadyrov, Ramzan 84–5
Kamotho, Joseph 105
Kane, Chief Inspector 157
Karr, John Mark 75
Kay, Assistant DA Steven 49
Kellerman, Mary 144
Kelly, Mary Jane 118
Kennedy, J. P. 18

Klein, William 193
Kleinszig, Manuela 58
Klosowski, Severin 119
Knight, Suge 76–7, 81
Kudimova, Elena 86
Kuklinski, Richard 212
Kurdish Workers' Party 63

L

Lewinsky, Monica 109
Lewis, James 147
Linares, Oscar Perez 52
Lincoln, Victoria 23
Litvinenko, Alexander 87
Long Island serial killer (LISK) 158–51
Los Rebeldes 68
Lowe, Harriet 124
Lowe, Sir Hudson 15
Lucan, John Bingham, 7th Earl 204–9
Lucan, Lady Veronica 204–5, 208

M

McCann, Madeleine 214–17
McDevitt, Brian 169
McFarland, Mary 145
McGurn, Jack 35–6, 37, 38, 39
McLoughlin, Sean 102
McPeake, John 33
Mafia 54–9, 126, 210–13
Mageau, Michael 134–5, 137, 138
Maggio, Joseph and Catherine 123

Maggiore, Brian and Katie 141
Makhmudov, Rustam 85
Malaysia Airlines Flight 17 110–13
Manning, Debra 142
Marcus, Constance 194
Marigny, Alfred de 41–2
Marref, Mohamed 189
Marx, Groucho 196
Maxwell-Scott, Susan 207, 208
May, John 36
Mbenna, Vella G. 105
Melchen, Captain Edward 43
Merlino, Carmello 167
Meza, Gonzalez 69
Mezzouar, Djelloul 189
Miyazaki, Manabu 162
Molina, Colonel Arturo 50
Montholon, Charles-Tristan de 15
Moran, George "Bugs" 34, 36
Moran, Dr. John 18, 21
Morey, Michael 169
Morris, Frank 198–200, 202
Morgan, J. P., Jr. 96
Morinaga and Co. 161–2
Morse, John Vinnicum 25
Muenter, Eric 96
Mumpre, Doc 127
Murray, Mick 102
Mystery Man with 21 Faces 160–3

N

Napoleon Bonaparte, Emperor 10–15

Ness, Eliot 130–1, 132
Nichols, Mary Ann 116

O

Oakes, Sir Harry 40–3
O'Brien, Barbara 197
O'Brien, Russell 215
Ocalan, Abdullah 63
Odeh, Mohamed Sadeek 107
Offerman, Dr. Robert 142, 143
Oldfield, Matt and Rachel 215
O'Neill, Denis "Sonny" 30–1
Original Night Stalker 140–3
al-'Owhali, Mohamed Rashed Daoud 107

P

P2 59
Palme, Lisbet 60–1, 62, 65
Palme, Olof 60–5
Pepitone, Esther 127
Pepitone, Mike 125, 127
Petersson, Krister 64
Pettersson, Gustav Christer 61–2
Pink Panthers 182–3
Pizer, John 118–19
Podracky, John 194
Poe, Edgar Allan 16–21
Poe, Elizabeth Ellicott 19
Polillo, Flo 130
Politkovskaya, Anna 82–87
Poparic, Milan 187
Price, Frank 200
Prince, Paula 145

Provenzano, Anthony 210, 211
Puff Daddy, see Combs, Sean
    "Puffy"
Putin, Vladimir 82, 84

R

Ramsey, Burke 70, 74
Ramsey, John and Patsy
    70–75
Ramsey, JonBenét 70–75
Reagan, Ronald 53
Reissfelder, George 167
Reynolds, Ruth 99
Ribeiro, Luiz Fernando 179
Ritz, Sally Lou 193
Rivett, Sandra 204, 206–7,
    208, 209
"The Rock" see Alcatraz
Rolfe, Louisa 38
Romano, Joseph 124
Romero, Archbishop Oscar
    50–3
Russell, Alice 27

S

St. Valentine's Day Massacre
    9, 34–9
Salish Sea feet mystery 88–91
Saravia, Captain Álvaro Rafael
    51, 52
Sazonoff, Jonathan 187
Scalise, John 37
Scarlett, Charles 21
Schiamba, Mrs. 123
Schneider, Edward 124
School of Turin 188
Schwimmer, Dr. Reinhart 36

Shackleton, Francis 157–8
Shakur, Tupac 76–81
Sharif, Abdul Latif 67–8
Sheeran, Frank 212
Shelton, Elmira 16, 19–20
Shepard, Cecelia Ann 136–7
Short, Elizabeth 44–9
Sickert, Walter 121
Sindicic, Vinko 65
Smalls, Biggie (Christopher
    Wallace) 77–81
Snodgrass, Joseph 17
Souza, Chagas 175
Stiltz, Jack 136
Stine, Paul 137
Stowell, Dr. Thomas 121
Stride, Elizabeth 118
Sullivan, Bridget 22–3
Sweeney, Dr. Francis 132

T

Tammany Hall 195
Tanner, Jane 215, 216
Terkibayev, Khanpash 87
Thompson, Laura 209
Turner, David 167
Tylenol Murders 144–7

U

Underwood, Agness "Aggie"
    46
United States Embassy
    bombing, East Africa 93,
    104–9
Uribe, García 69

V

Vicars, Sir Arthur 155, 156–7
Vittor, Silvano 56–7, 58

W

Walker, Joseph W. 16–17
Wall Street Bombing (1920)
    94–9
Wallace, Christopher, see
    Smalls, Biggie
Walsh, John Evangelist 19–20
Waterman, Megan 149
Weiner, Mary 145
Weinshank, Albert 36
West, Allen 199–200, 201
White, Fleet 71, 75
Wilson, James 208
Wilson, Vylla Poe 19
Windsor, Edward Duke of 43
Winkler, Georgette 37

Y

Yamamoto, Superintendent 163
Yushenkov, Sergei 87

Z

Zodiac Killer 134–9

IMAGE CREDITS